The Art of Clear Thinking:

Mental Models for Better Reasoning, Judgment, Analysis, and Learning. Upgrade Your Intellectual Toolkit.

By Patrick King
Social Interaction Specialist and
Conversation Coach
www.PatrickKingConsulting.com

Table of Contents

Table of Contents 5

Chapter 1. Intellectual Honesty 7
  The Armored Ego 11
  What is Intellectual Honesty (and Dishonesty)? 21
  Obstacles to Honest Thought 27
  On Forming Opinions 39

Chapter 2. (Don't) Trust Your Instincts 51
  Feelings Aren't Facts 54
  Perspective Isn't Reality 59
  Perception is Biased 66
  Memories are Wrong........................... 81
  The Laws of Logic 87

Chapter 3. The Open Mind 101
  Battle Confirmation Bias 108
  Follow the Evidence 116
  Battle Social Influence 125

Chapter 4. Greats Think Alike 141
  Elon Musk & SpaceX 142
  Darwin's Golden Rule 153
  Descartes, Doubt, and the Scientific Method 160

[Einstein and "What if?"](#) 169
[Socrates the Know-It-All](#) 176

Summary Guide 191

Chapter 1. Intellectual Honesty

The truth doesn't cost you anything, but a lie could cost you everything. - Unknown

What do we mean when we talk about *clear thinking*?

Given a minute or two to consider that question, most of us could come up with a definition related to intelligence. Usually, it depends on our goals at the moment.

Some might mix it up with *fast* thinking—where that happens automatically and often outside of our consciousness. Speed is prized over accuracy. They see a certain object or situation, and immediately draw a conclusion based on their own past experience out of urgency. Others might confuse it with *reactionary* thinking, which sounds like "my instincts are telling me this." It's establishing a belief based on an emotional hunch, which isn't thinking at all.

Or possibly, clear thinking is mixed up with *simple* thinking. Here, concepts that are easy to grasp are closer to the truth than more complicated ideas. This might happen because a clear solution is desired, and too much information can muddy the waters. On the other hand, the opposite confusion can hold true where clear thinking is seen as *complicated* thinking: analyzing every single bit of information, supporting and opposing, no matter how insignificant or questionable their sources may be.

All of us have practiced those kinds of thinking in the past and may have had confidence in our convictions based on them. Maybe even once or twice we've been *right* when using them. (Although it's probably the real life equivalent of a stopped clock being correct twice a day.)

Fast and reactionary thinking will help you when a car is hurtling your way and you aren't sure which way to leap; any direction is fine as long as it's safe. Simple thinking will help you when certainty is more valued than accuracy. Complicated thinking will help you when pedantry and accuracy are valued more than speed. But none of those mental models will reliably help you understand, learn about, and determine the truth of what's right in front of you.

Clear thinking is reasoning, determination based on evidence, critical analysis, and simply following the trail of cookie crumbs where it leads, not where you want it to lead or where you think it should lead. It emphasizes trying to find the objective truth and not being led astray by what we see at first glance. It is the magnifying glass that shows the important details that make all the difference, while tuning out those that are red herrings.

Adapting to clear thinking on a regular, practiced basis will help you become more understanding, perceptive, and insightful. Committing yourself to a deliberate and unbiased way of thinking is not necessarily about doing better in school or at your job—though it certainly aids those pursuits. It's mostly about viewing the world for what it is and being able to discern the naked truth of what you see.

There are elements of thinking like a scientist, gaining self-awareness of your own biases, and learning to be strict with yourself. It can be difficult, but you just may realize how flawed your thinking has been in the past. Not everybody is comes out of the womb thinking with crystal clarity, but everybody has the capacity to gain it as a habit.

This book intends to offer a set of principles and practices that will help you think more honestly and rationally. I hope to present clear thinking as a core component of your life that you need to instill; it's a skill that will reward you in virtually all aspects of your waking life. It's how you solve for actual solutions to your problems, instead of hoping that the clock happens to be right.

The first aspect of crystal-clear thinking is *intellectual honesty*, which is when you're honest with yourself and others, and your first obligation is to the pursuit of truth rather than any other motive.

We frequently lie to others when we want to protect ourselves from their judgment. For instance, if someone makes fun of your writing skills, you'll utter an excuse about how you were distracted, lazy, and not putting in your full effort. Also, your computer was on the fritz that day, so you couldn't perform any editing. *Sure.* This type of reaction is not intellectually honest, but it's understandable and natural.

But what happens when you begin to tell the same lies to yourself, and you are unable to tell where the truth begins or ends? What if you start to believe that you're an undiscovered Ernest Hemingway, but for your laziness and broken keyboard? That is the true risk with a lack of intellectual honesty, and it presents a huge obstacle to clarity of thought and staying rooted in reality.

The Armored Ego

As you just saw with the example about your writing prowess, protecting yourself from others is often the reason we are intellectually dishonest. In fact, the first barrier in almost *any* kind of self-improvement comes from the ego's need to protect itself. Sometimes our thinking is erroneous because we don't see all the factors involved in a situation, or we are too hasty to jump to a conclusion. Those are errors in observation or perception. But those reasons pale in comparison to the ego's power to distort your thinking.

Someone who's underperforming at work might feel the need to protect their perceived skills and talent by deflecting responsibility to "The boss has always had it in for me. And who trained me? Him! It's all his fault one way or another." Someone who trips and falls yet fancies themselves graceful will blame the fact that it rained six days ago, their shoes have no grip, and *who put that rock there anyway!*? Someone who fails to make the school basketball team will grumble that the coach hated them, they weren't used to that particular style of play, and they didn't *really* want to make the team anyway.

This is what it sounds like when the ego steps in to protect itself. There's so much justification and deflecting going on that it's difficult to know what is real and what is not. Clear thinking becomes impossible.

This all stems from the universal truth that nobody likes to be wrong or to fail. It's embarrassing and confirms all of our worst anxieties about ourselves. Instead of accepting being wrong as a teachable moment or lesson, our first instinct is to run from our shame and cower in the corner. This is the same reason we will persist in an argument to the death, even if we know we are 100% wrong. If the ego had a physical manifestation, it would be sizable, sensitive, and heavily armored (to the point of going on the offensive)—essentially a giant porcupine.

When the ego senses danger, it has no interest or time to consider the facts. Instead it seeks to alleviate your discomfort in the quickest way possible. And that means you lie to yourself so you can keep the ego safe and sound.

We try to cover up the truth, deflect attention from it, or develop an alternative version that makes the actual truth seem less hurtful. And it's right in that moment that intellectual dishonesty is born. Are any of those convoluted theories likely to withstand any amount of scrutiny? Probably not, but the problem is that the ego doesn't allow for acknowledgment and analysis of what really happened. It blinds you.

Let's be clear: These aren't lies that you dream up or concoct in advance. You do not *intend* to lie to yourself. You don't even *feel* they're lies. You may not even know you're doing it, as sometimes these defense mechanisms can occur unconsciously. They're not explicitly intellectually dishonest because you *want* to delude yourself. Rather, they're automatic strategies that the constantly neurotic ego puts into action because it's terrified of looking foolish or wrong. Unfortunately, that's the worst zone to be in, as it means *you don't know what you don't know.*

Over time these ego-driven errors in thinking inform your entire belief system and give you rationalized justifications for almost everything. You never make any sports team because the coaches always hate you, and you keep failing the driving test because your hand-eye coordination is *uniquely special.*

These lies become your entire reality, and you rely on them to get yourself through problematic situations or to dismiss efforts to find the truth. We're not talking about just giving excuses for why you aren't a violin virtuoso; this manner of thinking can become the factors that drive your decisions, thinking, and evaluations of anything and anyone.

Let's take Fred. Fred was an ardent fan of a pop star his whole life. He grew up listening to their music and formed a lot of his identity around his admiration for him. We're talking an entire bedroom wall filled with posters of this star, and outfits that were replicas of this star's clothes hanging in his closet.

Late in his career this pop star was put on trial for a serious crime. Fred steadfastly stood by his pop star idol, even as lurid details of his case were reported by courtroom reporters to the press. "Nobody I admire this way would ever be guilty of this," Fred said. "It's all just a conspiracy put together by the people who resent him for whatever reason."

The pop star was ultimately found guilty and sentenced to multiple years of prison. Fred had showed up outside the courthouse bearing a sign that protested his star's innocence. Even as compelling evidence was eventually released to the press, Fred maintained that the pop star was absolutely innocent, dismissing all of the victims' claims by protesting that they were "jealous" and "just trying to get the spotlight themselves."

Why would Fred continue to insist, against all reasonable and provable evidence, that his idol was innocent? Because his ego was so wrapped up in his worship of the pop star that it was predisposed to consider him blameless. For him to believe the truth would have meant a devastating blow to almost everything he believed in (*I worship a criminal? What does that say about me?),* and the ego wasn't going to let that happen for a minute—even if it meant making him deny what was fairly compelling and unshakable proof that the star was guilty.

In your pursuit of truth and clear thought, your ego will rear its ugly head like the enraged porcupine. It has set up a series of tactical barriers to keep you from learning something that might upset your belief system, and it is only after you can reign in your ego that you are open to learning. After all, you can't defend yourself and listen at the same time.

Defense mechanisms are the specific ways we protect our ego, pride, and self-esteem. These methods keep us whole when times are tough. The origin of the term comes from Sigmund Freud. You just might recognize these two defense mechanisms put forth by his daughter, Anna Freud: denial and rationalization.

Denial is one of the most classic defense mechanisms because it is easy to use. Suppose you discovered that you were performing poorly at your job. "No, I don't believe that report ranking all of the employees. There's no way I can be last. Not in this world. The computer added up the scores incorrectly."

What is true is simply claimed to be false, as if that makes everything go away. You are acting as if a negative fact doesn't exist. Sometimes we don't realize when we do this, especially in situations that are so dire they actually appear fantastical to us.

All you have to do is say "no" often enough and you might begin to believe yourself, and that's where the appeal of denial lies. You are actually changing your reality, where other defense mechanisms merely spin it to be more acceptable. This is actually the most dangerous defense mechanism, because even if there is a dire problem, it is ignored and never fixed. If someone continued to persist in the belief they were an excellent driver, despite a string of accidents in the past year, it's unlikely they would ever seek to practice their driving skills.

Rationalization is when you explain away something negative.

It is the art of making excuses. The bad behavior or fact still remains, but it is turned into something unavoidable because of circumstances out of your control. The bottom line is anything negative is not your fault and you shouldn't be held accountable for it. It's never a besmirching of your abilities. It's extremely convenient, and you are only limited by your imagination.

Building on the same prior example of poor job performance, this is easily explained away by the following: your boss secretly hating you, your co-workers plotting against you, the computer being biased against your soft skills, unpredictable traffic affecting your commute, and having two jobs at once. These flimsy excuses are what your ego needs to protect itself.

Rationalization is the embodiment of the *sour grapes fable*: A fox wanted to reach some grapes at the top of a bush, but he couldn't leap high enough. To make himself feel better about his lack of leaping ability, and to comfort himself about his lack of grapes, he told himself the grapes looked sour anyway, so he wasn't missing out on anything. He was still hungry, but he'd rather be hungry than admit his failure.

Rationalization can also help us feel at peace with poor decisions we've made with phrases such as, "It was going to happen at some point anyway." Rationalization ensures you never have to face failure, rejection, or negativity. It's always someone else's fault!

While comforting, where do reality and truth go amidst all of this? Out the window, mostly. Intellectual honesty requires you to first defeat your natural tendencies to be dishonest. Thoughts dictated by self-protection don't overlap with clear, objective thoughts.

What is Intellectual Honesty (and Dishonesty)?

With our biggest obstacle addressed, it's time to examine the traits of the honest thinking we want to seek out. And what are the traits of *dishonest* thinking that we want to avoid? It's time to spell out how to embody our goals of seeing the world as objectively as humanly possible.

Intellectual honesty is a commitment to finding the truth, wholly, unconditionally, no matter what it might cost. It's seeking out facts and reality, regardless of how uneasy, inopportune or distasteful that truth makes us feel. Often it involves what our ego would rather pretend doesn't exist. It is the understanding that speed and certainty are completely unimportant when compared to accuracy.

The intellectually honest person is tireless about learning from all perspectives. They accept viewpoints that might differ from their own. They understand that reasonable people can hold opposing ideas. They're swift in respecting the good points their opponents might bring up, and they're not afraid to admit when their own argument might contain flaws or faults. They're quick to concede when their own biases, prejudices or emotions might be informing their thinking.

Someone who's committed to intellectual honesty is committed to the absolute facts of a matter and allows those facts alone to form their judgment. They don't exaggerate or overstate arguments, and they don't deliberately misconstrue what evidence presents them. They don't make the truth adapt to their thinking. There is no circuitous logic or circular arguments, and questions are answered directly and without ulterior motive. If the ego senses danger, it acts swiftly to make most people spout an excuse, but the intellectually honest will throw themselves under the bus if that accurately reflects what happened.

The intellectually honest person remains modest and neutral when they're pursuing the truth. They reject double standards and hypocrisy, and they don't pretend to be experts on things they don't know anything about. For example, a courtroom judge is expected to ignore their own personal beliefs, withstand outside pressure, and make an unbiased decision on cases or procedures completely adherent to the rule of law. The evidence will tell a story, and the judge removes their own opinions, gives each side the same opportunity, and simply uncovers that story instead of seeking to write it themselves.

An insurance adjustor investigating an accident, theoretically speaking, needs to block out both his company's bottom line and their customer's adverse situation, examine all the facts and events of the accident, and make their best judgment as to how it happened and which party is responsible. He is to assess according to the guidelines he is bound by, nothing more and nothing less. He cannot skip analyzing something because it is damaging to his company's bottom line, and he must give the same weight to every factor he finds.

There is an element of scientific thinking, where a hypothesis or assumption is something that is meant to be tested, and is certainly never confused with a conclusion or argument. "I don't know" is a perfectly acceptable answer, and so is "You're right, I am wrong." Each option is equally comfortable and easy to speak.

An intellectually *dishonest* person, on the other hand, is often easily identified by how they react to anything that doesn't support them. They either don't accept hostile to opposing opinions through denial or rationalization, or are downright hostile and demeaning. You just get the sense that there is something to be protected or hidden. They evade questions like they are playing dodge ball, and they come up with roundabout answers to direct inquiries. Thoughts focused on being right don't always overlap with reality or the truth.

When it comes to reinforcing their own beliefs, the intellectually dishonest person stops their research the minute they find something that supports their assertion.

They'll cherry-pick evidence they agree with and completely omit proof that they're wrong. They'll mangle the truth until it suits them by making bad analogies, taking quotes out of context, and equivocating or minimizing key points. They'll go off on tangents to misrepresent the facts of a situation, in some cases simply making stuff up to support their statements. Using straw man arguments is a favorite: these are fallacies in which one arguer exaggerates what their opponent said to the point of ludicrous, when in actuality that opponent said nothing of the sort.

Innocent statement: "Maybe we should trust our government more."

Straw man argument: "Oh, so you're saying you want a fascist government and our very own Hitler to go along with?!"

"...No, that's not what I said at all."

When they sense their argument is disbelieved, the intellectually dishonest person often resorts to panic, distortion, or deflection. The discussion becomes something to win, and they do it by any means possible. They'll exaggerate, misinterpret, cry false equivalencies, or simply change the subject. Defense becomes the name of the game. There is an inability to answer yes or no questions without having to justify; there is never a straightforward answer given.

Over time, an intellectually dishonest person can lob so many of these defenses and tactics so often and repetitively that they even talk themselves *into* believing something they used to know wasn't entirely on solid ground to begin with. Like abiding by the ego, the most dangerous side effect of intellectual dishonesty is the potential to warp reality on a mass scale.

As mentioned earlier, we engage in self-deceptions out of self-defense. But furthermore, nothing is quite as narcotic as the need to be right; and to maintain that feeling, we lie to ourselves.

Switching from a track of intellectual dishonesty to one of clear thinking isn't a cakewalk. It requires leaving behind established beliefs and biases that are difficult to let go of. In the process, you leave yourself feeling vulnerable and inadequate. Uttering, "I don't know" or "I was wrong" for the first time can be painful. But consider that the bravado and bluster you showcase in intellectual dishonesty paints a far worse picture of you.

Obstacles to Honest Thought

Our egos play a large part in obscuring clear and critical thought, but even if you are able to quash it and eventually separate your thinking processes from it, there are still many habits that cloud our thinking. Just like dealing with the ego, they might be so habitual and heavily ingrained that you can't find the truth with a compass.

The three common obstacles are intellectual laziness, willful ignorance, and adherence to sacred cows. They each impact our ability to see truth in different ways.

Intellectual laziness. Especially in today's technology-driven society where answers are easier and quicker to obtain than ever before, we tend to expend very little energy into intellectual pursuits. Our brains seek the fastest of superficial confirmations of facts and then head straight for the beach for a few hours. The goal is ease and certainty rather than accuracy. It's easy and it feels like you've done what you're supposed to. This in itself leads to chronic jumping to conclusions.

But there's more to an intellectually lazy person than just seeking comfort. They prefer that other people do the thinking for them. They'll happily defer to the beliefs of a friend, social media memes, or dubious experts to define their convictions. They outsource their critical thinking and seek to substitute it with apparent authority figures, which inevitably leave large gaps of understanding. You have to wonder at what point they are creating their own opinions instead of parroting what they have heard from often-questionable sources.

Aside from not being discerning with sources, the intellectually lazy person also doesn't want to take the effort to change their mind, and they'll pursue that stasis to the ends of the earth. In the pursuit of maintaining consistency over seeking truth, they'll only consider information that will back up what they *want* to believe, whether it's debunked science or a far-flung conspiracy theory. Even if they're presented with clear evidence and reasoning, they'll refuse to consider any of it, or reject it out of hand without understanding a single part of it.

They seek the path of least resistance. As such, they over-value stability, and are resistant to change. Saying "I don't know" is not preferred because it requires extra work to juggle multiple perspectives—it's not an easy, comfortable state. It's much easier to be able to latch onto one opinion or perspective.

When an intellectually lazy person *does* take the mantle and try to do their own research, they'll often stop after a cursory glance—and even then, they'll probably only look at material that supports their own beliefs. They seek to oversimplify and remove nuance from complex issues. After all, it's more effort to have to understand your errors and change your perspective. If they get backed into a corner by someone rationally challenging their views, you just might see the ego start to rear its ugly head.

Like all the other aspects of clear thinking, avoiding intellectual laziness becomes an exercise in building habits of self-awareness and metacognition—thinking about your own thinking.

Ask yourself if you are merely seeking an answer or if you are actually seeking the truth. These different paths prescribe incredibly different courses of action. To see truth, you don't stop researching something the minute you find your viewpoints (or their opposites) validated. You seek information from as many sides and sources as you can and accept that some real evidence you come across might make you uncomfortable.

You would engage in this search firsthand, as opposed to listening to other people's anecdotes. You would seek to discover nuance and not settle at the first explanation that seems plausible. You would treat your assumptions as just that, assumptions and not fact or truth. It sounds exhausting, but the more you use these muscles, the easier it gets.

Willful ignorance. It's one thing to be intellectually dishonest through mental laziness and prioritizing your comfort over the truth, but it's quite another thing to *know* you're relying on faulty information, mislead others, but keep on doing it anyway. This is called willful ignorance, and it's worse than mere intellectual laziness.

Willful ignorance is making a deliberate choice to disregard the truth. Examples include the conspiracy theorist who won't consider any information that exposes the holes in their argument, like people in the '60s who thought Paul McCartney was dead, and rejected clear evidence like his giving new television interviews frequently ("It was an imposter!") and releasing new music ("It was the *same* imposter!").

But willful ignorance happens in less fringe situations as well: In the 1990s, when tobacco companies knew that science had proven their product was harmful, they fought to suppress the data and deny its authority by claiming it was "inconclusive." If you assume that tobacco companies weren't knowingly poisoning their customers, they turned a blind eye to compelling evidence simply because they wanted to believe it so badly. It's the equivalent of plugging your ears, covering your eyes, and loudly screaming "LA-LA-LA-LA-LA" to deny something.

There's more than innocent ignorance behind those that practice willful ignorance: They consciously opt to spurn the truth, with statements ranging from the relatively benign ("It's none of my business") to the dismissive ("I don't want to know"). Such brazen refusal is usually a sign that the speaker knows there's something wrong with their position and merely wants to escape the proceedings.

Several reasons might be at play when someone displays willful ignorance. Remember, denial typically serves the ego. They could just be insecure about their beliefs and want to avoid information that would conflict with them. They may want to escape the responsibility to change that comes with new knowledge—to paraphrase the Jack Nicholson movie quote, they "can't handle the truth!" Alternately, they may simply perceive ignorance as the psychologically healthier option: They prefer to "stay positive" and preserve the relative tranquility of "not knowing."

This harms you because without the truth, and without acknowledging your possible role in it, improvement is impossible. It's like when the "Check Engine" light goes on in one's car. They can rationalize it away by saying, "Oh, that light goes on all the time. It's irrelevant." Then they continue to ignore it, until one night they try to start the car and it won't turn over. More personally, we see willful ignorance when someone refuses to acknowledge hard evidence that their partner might not be totally truthful with them, continuing to stick silently by their side thinking things will get better by just pretending nothing's wrong.

Knowing that your beliefs or facts don't align with reality is *important.* Willful ignorance is short-circuited by making the simple yet tough decision to start with facts and then find a conclusion, instead of starting with the conclusion and then finding the facts to support it.

Some reading this will find the risks of losing willful ignorance too much to endure. Still others will say there's nothing wrong with being willfully ignorant if it makes them happy. But don't confuse this comfort zone for clear thinking.

Adherence to sacred cows. Certain subjects, ideas, people or groups are considered by some to be off-limits when it comes to criticism or even critical analysis. These items are called "sacred cows," in reference to the Hindu belief that the cow is a holy animal that must not be eaten or disrespected.

Discussing sacred cows can be extremely problematic, because they speak directly to people's core of faith, belief and identity. For our purposes, sacred cows can include anything from long-established cultural traditions, religious practices, political beliefs, and even industry practices. Anything that is held out to be the unquestionable truth, or above truth itself, is a sacred cow. In everyday terms, they are "touchy subjects."

To say anything critical of those hallowed institutions and figures is considered blasphemy by those who follow them. But *are* they accurate, truthful, and deserving of such a label? What gives them their status, and what makes them more correct than anything else? Is it simply a result of "doing things for the sake of doing them as they have always been done"?

To be clear, this is not a point about discussing the merits of the Hindu belief regarding the cow. This is a point about questioning your beliefs and separating long-held assumption from fact.

Intellectually honesty dictates that no subject, belief, or person should be free from critical thinking or questioning. If you honestly engage in this process, sooner or later you're going to step directly onto someone's sacred cow, even your own. This is when you encounter something that you believed to be incontrovertible truth, and when you come into conflict with that, how will you react? Will you be able to follow the evidence where it leads, or ignore it by deferring to your sacred cow?

But it's a dangerous discussion. It sparks intense defensiveness. Centuries of chaos and bloodshed have resulted from these attitudes. You might have your own internal battles on the matter. As with many things in life, discomfort here is a sign of something significant occurring.

There is no tenet or belief that should be accepted completely on blind faith. Every single one of them should be open to scrutiny and investigation. The best ideas and principles will stand up to such inquiry—the truth will always be defensible. Only beliefs that rely on falsehoods, outdated thought or misinformation will lose out.

Imagine that you (after having traveled through time) are working diligently to construct a theory on whether or not the planets orbit the sun, or everything orbits the Earth. You may recognize this as the debate between heliocentrism and geocentrism, respectively. Geocentrism was indeed considered a sacred cow. Where would we be if it wasn't taken off its pedestal and intensely questioned and ultimately proven incorrect by Nicolaus Copernicus?

If you have a sacred cow, the biggest step is to at least recognize and admit that it is a sacred cow rather than a fact. People are free to believe what they want, but they are not free to present what they want as truth or fact.

This idea is behind the famous Zen teaching of Linji Yixuan: "*If you meet the Buddha on the road, kill him.*" This means that one shouldn't be so beholden to knowledge of a certain person or belief system, and if they have the opportunity, to destroy it or them to gain clarity of thought.

What are your sacred cows? Why do you consider them sacrosanct and beyond reproach?

- What beliefs or subjects are off-limits with you?

- What are you unwilling to be critical of or criticize?

- What are you unwilling to discuss honestly without growing defensive?

- What do you feel must not be questioned?

Take time to question and at least identify them. The goal isn't to change your mind about your beliefs, it's just to gain a better understanding of what your beliefs are built upon. That actually may *strengthen* your beliefs. But don't be afraid or panicked if doubt creeps in—investigate that too. You're not betraying yourself if you do that; you're using your brain for its intended purpose. Questioning your sacred cows isn't about being disrespectful or rude, it's about knowing that the truth fears no questions, nor does it need you to defend it any more than gravity, logic, or mathematics needs you to defend them.

On Forming Opinions

"Opinions are like mouths, everyone has one." Have you ever heard this phrase, or a more vulgar version? It means that opinions are natural to have and inescapable. However, this doesn't say anything about their accuracy or the unfortunate consequence that many people like to substitute their opinions for fact.

Sound opinions can only come from intellectual honesty. Especially in the times we live, when it seems like it's more important to have loud and quickly-delivered beliefs, going out of your way to take deliberate steps in establishing your views is vital.

Philosopher Bertrand Russell identified some of the pitfalls of making hasty opinions, as outlined in one of the essays that comprised his anthology *The Basic Writings of Bertrand Russell*. He may not have known it at the time, but he was one of intellectual honesty's first proponents. His approach was to ensure that they aren't clouded by sentiment, bias, or corrupt thinking. Accordingly, one of Russell's lasting legacies is the work he did in the philosophy of logic, which first started with Aristotle.

"If the matter is one that can be settled by observation, make the observation yourself." It's one thing to believe facts and opinions that you've read or heard about, and there are some that you can even take for granted. You're secure in believing that bears hibernate in winter, even if you've never personally tracked a bear as he's preparing to pack it in for the season. Is it possible for you to observe them yourself? Other people have, and it might be safe to take their word on it for this one if you trust them.

When you can—especially when it comes to opinions—you should try out your beliefs yourself. If you believe that a new shopping center near your kid's school is creating heavy and unsafe traffic when school lets out, take a day or two to actually watch and measure the traffic on the street to back up your opinion. Can it truly be *your* opinion if you don't have a basis for it?

Don't just take others' opinions for your own, no matter how persuasive your sources. It's a mistake to assert that you know something when you don't. The more strongly you believe something, the higher the risk that you're being swayed by personal bias. If you have a chance to test your beliefs, take it.

"If a contrary opinion makes you angry, you might subconsciously know you have no good reason for your thinking." The most volatile blow-ups we have in intellectual discourse occur when we're discussing matters that are, at heart, unprovable. We don't get angry when we hear a math equation; "2 plus 2 equals 4" will not make someone fly into a vicious rage unless they're extremely unstable. It's subjective matters of the spirit that people clash over, be it theology, favorite music styles, or whether their favorite sports team "sucks."

If you find yourself getting increasingly angry when you're in a debate with someone, stop and think why you're getting incensed. Russell suggests that you may subliminally know that your viewpoint isn't necessarily backed up by the strongest proof, and you are dreading the inevitable feeling of being wrong. The more agitated and hotter you are about defending yourself, the higher the chance that you're standing on shaky intellectual ground. If the ego is awakening, there just might be a reason.

"Become aware of opinions outside your social circle." In fact, seek them out. Many times we adopt certain beliefs because our friends and family believe them. For all intents and purposes, those opinions become our reality. Then, we fear being ostracized or rejected by the social circles we're in if we dare express a countering viewpoint. Other times we may sincerely hold those opinions but have no visibility into what a counterpoint might look or sound like. Echo chambers are where strict, dictatorial stances are left free to develop and turn into ruthless dogma.

Seek out the viewpoints of people far outside your immediate group of friends. Don't argue against them or refute them. Listen. Read or watch the news sources of the opponent if you can't get out and talk to them personally. Understand that people live in different worlds, despite walking or sitting right next to you on the subway.

In many cases you'll find they might have some good points. And if you still find their views repugnant or unhealthy—well, that's how they feel about *you*. As unlikely as it seems, exposure to the opposition is the best way to find common ground, decrease intolerance, and balance your own opinions.

On a related note, after gaining a bit of understanding of other people, try engaging in the thought exercise of how someone with an alternate perspective might respond to your opinions. There may be zero chance that you actually change your mind on certain things, but at least you've gained perspective and hopefully empathy.

"Be wary of opinions that flatter your self-esteem." Any politician will tell you that the best way to instill a belief in a certain individual is to appeal to their ego. They win over crowds by complimenting their patriotism, emotions and overall profile.

This should be self-evident—people don't get *insulted* into believing a certain way, but they *can* be cajoled and seduced into it.

But just because a vendor calls you beautiful or handsome doesn't mean the price of that jacket will fit your bank account. Beware when you're hearing an opinion from someone that makes you feel validated and righteous all over. Is it honest, or is it pandering and flattering for the purpose of gaining compliance? There's a chance it's formed and delivered in such a way that you can't *help* but be manipulated or charmed into believing it. No matter how sound or rational the opinion might be, check to make sure it's as appealing to your intellect more than your sense of pride. Thinking clearly means going more deeply than your emotional reactions.

For Russell, forming opinions is not something to be taken lightly, and a certain amount of responsibility comes with it. Others may not engage in this process, but that doesn't mean you shouldn't.

Charlie Munger, the businessman and philanthropist who is best known as financial partner to Warren Buffett, once said, "I never allow myself to have an opinion on anything that I don't know the other side's argument better than they do." That view goes hand in hand with Russell's directives above to seek ideas outside your social circle and imagine how someone would argue back to you. Don't just come up with a bullet list of counteracting opinions—go deeply into the opposition's point of view. You should become your own toughest and most articulate critic.

We're not programmed to do this instinctively. The brain has a strong inclination to confirmation bias, the tendency to only hear opinions that support our own viewpoints that we'll explore later. But ours is a brain that is programmed for a combination of speed and certainty, not accuracy. Acting decisively in the face of a speeding truck can save your life, while trying to determine truth can leave you a splatter on the road. But that's not the situation we are dealing with, is it? In the absence of threats to your life, truth should always be the end goal, and opinions should be formed only after making an honest effort to pursue it.

"Strong opinions which are lightly held" is a helpful rule of thumb. Have certainty in what you know, but also be open to what you don't know and how it impacts your current opinion. Make your opinion a reflection of what you currently know, and keep updating it to adapt. When you don't attach to a particular opinion, you'll find that truth becomes easier and easier to see as well as find. If you do feel an attachment, it's probably a sign that you are not being guided by intellectual honesty.

Takeaways:

- If you reflect for a second, clear thinking is not usually the goal we have in mind. We are usually after a combination of quick, simple, or easy thinking. However, none of those things are particularly *accurate* and won't lead you to the answers you seek. Unfortunately, it's what we are wired to do, and it takes conscious effort to slow down and be thorough. Most of the time, we also want to quell our sense of uncertainty, which leads us to conclusions that, while speedy, are not focused on accuracy. Intellectual honesty is about seeking plain and unadulterated truth.

- One of clear thinking's biggest opponents is the ego. This is when an argument, stance, or opinion is supported not by evidence, but by pride, the need to be right, and the desire to avoid shame and embarrassment. Ego keeps us deaf and blind if we allow it to. It serves a purpose, but very quickly becomes detrimental to your evaluation of the world, as it has the power to warp reality around you. The most prominent defense mechanisms we use are rationalization and plain old denial.

- Along with the ego, there are a few notable obstacles to pursuing truth and clarity of thought. They are intellectual laziness (*I can't be bothered to understand or research this, so I will accept anything*), willful ignorance (*I reject and deny that there is something further to understand*), and adherence to sacred cows (*that topic or stance is simply irrefutable truth; I refuse to question it*).

- It's easy to tell someone who is intellectually honest versus dishonest. It's all about how arguments contrary to their view are processed. The intellectually honest focus on understanding and following the evidence where it leads. The intellectually dishonest focus on a narrative that they want to preserve, and become defensive and sometimes outright hostile. The intellectually honest are able to answer questions directly and without justification; the intellectually dishonest must provide explanations, roundabouts, and deflections. Usually, it's clear that there is something being substituted for evidence that shouldn't be.

- Having an opinion is something we all do, but we must recognize that we often do it based on insufficient information and questionable evidence. An opinion is one thing, while forming a well-founded and defensible opinion is quite another. The latter, as Bertrand Russell writes, requires that you be wary of opinions which flatter your self-esteem. Imagine different biases and perspectives, look outside your immediate social circle, and question why an opposing opinion might make you react emotionally. It can be summed up with "Strong opinions which are lightly held."

Chapter 2. (Don't) Trust Your Instincts

There are three things extremely hard: steel, a diamond, and to know one's self. - Benjamin Franklin

Humans tend to place a lot of value on *instinct*. Especially as the pace of modern life forces us at times to think quickly on our feet and make immediate decisions, we believe that having superior *instinct* helps us get along. That's certainly true to an extent. But the problem is that sometimes we confuse instinct as a substitute for good judgment. However, instinct and good judgment are entirely separate things. Instinct may sometimes result overlap with good judgment, but they are not interchangeable.

Good judgment comes through a process of experience over time. Just as the Grand Canyon was created through an incredibly long process, good judgment requires a similar amount of refinement and progress. Only then can you develop a sense of intuition that is likely to lead to an accurate and helpful answer.

Good judgment is invariably balanced and thorough. Neither of those words describes our instincts.

Instincts are otherwise known as gut feelings or hunches, and, unless you are the literary detective known as Sherlock Holmes, are probably wrong the vast majority of the time. Instinct by definition is evaluating based on limited information. It turns out that when we make quick decisions based on instinct, we are usually jumping to conclusions and not seeing the whole picture. We already know that humans are predisposed to prefer speed and certainty over accuracy, and that's why it's so important to act against what your instincts want to tell you.

In addition to being Sherlock Holmes, unless you have the eye of an eagle, the ears of a rabbit, and the nose of a bloodhound, there's just no way your instinct is going to be correct on a consistent basis.

Let's take the field of cooking to illustrate the difference. An experienced chef will be able to use his judgment, based on years of experience, to design a menu that will be versatile and tasty. He will be able to do this time after time, through a variety of different cuisines. Compare this to the instincts of a neophyte chef. On rare occasions, the neophyte chef's menu might be preferable because there is an overlap between instinct and good judgment. But instinct is going to fail him in the long run without deeper knowledge.

We are biologically programmed to go with the first thought that pops into our head, which is a recipe for disaster. This chapter covers how to overcome the traps that come from relying on that initial flood of certainty in many ways, from our emotions, perspective, perception, and even memories. This will involve creating psychological distance from yourself to stop acting against your own interests.

Feelings Aren't Facts

One common error that all of us have made at some point in our lives is interpreting our emotional responses as truth—that is, confusing our feelings for facts. We observe or experience a situation that causes certain feelings to stir, and we interpret them not as subjective interpretations, but tangible reality.

This is otherwise known as emotional reasoning, and it is the polar opposite of clear thought. In emotional reasoning, you agree with the following statement: "I feel this way, therefore it must be true." If you feel negatively about a certain person, they must be terrible people. If you feel optimistically about a test, it must be easy. If you feel doubtful about a promise, the person on the other side of the promise must be scheming something. Emotions, both mild and intense, create an altered reality.

It's often a process that evades our conscious thought, which makes it tough to spot.

On one hand, it shouldn't be surprising that emotions can disrupt our thinking so powerfully. Emotions have overlapping purposes with instincts; they are both "act first, analyze later" types of thinking, and this is something that's kept us alive as a species. Both emotions and instinct were designed to be able to short circuit our brains and push analytical thought out of the way in favor of action.

While engaging in this behavior, observed evidence is discarded in favor of the truth of your feelings about the event. Emotional reasoning is one of the most dangerous obstacles to clear thought because it can be so wildly different from reality and can change in the span of minutes. Is reality actually changing moment by moment? Of course not! Only your emotions are changing that quickly.

Just like you wouldn't go grocery shopping when hungry, you shouldn't evaluate anything when emotional. Always take time to return to a calm state before making decisions or committing yourself to a specific course of action.

Reality is neutral, and it is your emotions that cause you to perceive it in any particular way. Viewing a situation with emotional reasoning is like watching a completely benign scene with horror music being played over it. And then joyous music. And then the next minute, music fitting for a clown's entrance. Now compound this with the act that everyone has a different soundtrack playing over the same scene. You won't know what's really happening in front of your face because the music will influence you a certain way. The only hope you have is to *turn off the music*—by removing emotions from the equation as best you can.

Phobias are a prime example of how we confuse facts and feelings. An agoraphobic has a fear of outside or open places that offer no immediate escape route. There's no established factual basis for this kind of fear, especially since there are so many people who *aren't* agoraphobic. Sure, bad things *can* happen to someone when they're outside the home, but the huge majority of the time they don't. But an agoraphobic's fear has irrationally turned itself into a fact in their mind; therefore, they're not leaving the house anytime soon.

Those who interpret feeling as facts have it completely backward. Our emotions are *products* of our thoughts. They are how we decide to interpret what we experience based on the observations and information we've received from the world around us.

I'm not suggesting you *not* have feelings—that's impossible. But you can and should treat your feelings like every other bit of information you receive. It should be *one* factor into how you think and evaluate situations and people. There might be a reason you are feeling a certain emotion; it might also exist because of entirely unrelated matters. The simple truth is that when we are emotionally invested, we lack the proper perspective to think clearly. Think of it as standing too close to a brick wall such that you can't see the entire building, only a singular brick. You'd need distance to see reality.

Focus on separating your emotional reaction from your actual response. Feel the first emotional reaction and label it as drastic and emotionally influenced. Let it pass or dissipate. Now, begin to dissect it. Only at this point can you think clearly and rationally. Of course, it has to be mentioned that this isn't a point on becoming a cold, calculating robot—although for our purposes of clear thinking, there could be worse things.

This is a point to make sure you aren't being controlled by emotion, which is not based on evidence or what's in front of you—it's based on past experiences, assumptions, or unfair associations. Feel your feelings—sometimes they are a signal for something that you don't consciously perceive, which is why they shouldn't be totally discounted—but don't become overwhelmed by them. Also beware that people are triggers for strong emotions, and this can distort reality even more than usual.

Perspective Isn't Reality

Now that we've articulated that feelings aren't facts, it's time to discuss another instance where your first impression will lead you astray. It's also another instance that can be characterized as "what you see is *not* what you get."

We can begin with a fable of sorts that you may have heard before. It's the fable of the six blind men and the elephant. These six blind men happened to surround an elephant one day. How they ended up there is not important, but if you require a backstory, pretend that they are on a surprise field trip with their scrabble team. Now, elephants are quite large, which means each blind man was situated at a different part of the elephant. One by one, they reached out to the part of the elephant that was nearest to them: the knee, the side, the tusk, the trunk, the ear, and the tail.

What followed was mass confusion. Even though it was one animal, each man had only his sense of touch to discern what he was standing by. From the descriptions they each gave, it was as if they were standing in completely different ecosystems, much less touching a different animal. An elephant ear can feel like the wing of a bat, the side can feel like a rhino, the tusk can feel like a building, and the trunk can feel like a tree trunk swaying in the wind. Six different positions yielded six different perspectives.

The thing is, none of these blind men were actually wrong, but their perspectives were limited by what they could feel in their positions, to the point that they ended up being incredibly wrong about the elephant's overall appearance.

Perspective is not reality, it's just *your* perspective, and you must gain a three-dimensional view of a situation or decision in order to be able to think clearly about it. Whether you want to admit it or not, we are all some version of the six blind men, only feeling what's in front of us, and not being able to conceive of what we might be missing.

For a more direct illustration, just imagine that for two people standing across from each other, the number 6 drawn in chalk at their feet is also a 9 (or is it the other way around?).

There's no right or wrong way to perceive a given situation or object. Our ideas, images and opinions of life are all subject to molding through our experiences. Nobody has a foolproof, 100% objective way to perceive reality accurately. However, there is a *complete* way to view things, and it necessarily involves as many perspectives as possible.

Take a man and a woman walking out of a motel in the middle of the afternoon in slightly disheveled clothes.

Some of us would have zero impression because we are too distracted and busy. A moral crusader might assume that they were having an afternoon fling that is intended to be kept secret from their significant others. Someone who works in an adult industry might be so desensitized to such a sighting that it barely registers to them at all. Meanwhile someone who works as a travel agent may not even consider what the couple were doing in their room; they'll wonder how much they paid for the room and what rating they would give it. And the motel housekeeper probably just cares about how much of a mess they're going to clean up.

The point is, we can take a moment as minuscule and unimportant as this one and run with it, making assumptions, predictions, or judgments that may be completely inaccurate, simply because of what we know (or, more accurately, what we *think* we know). We do this based on our character, values or experiences. And it's a natural and nearly unpreventable thing to do. But it's not reality.

Any number of things shape our interpretations of events and situations in the world. Our religious, political or philosophical leanings can shape how we see the world. So can our childhood upbringings. So can drugs or alcohol usage.

So can the media. So can our social or institutional environment. So can our fondness for cats or dogs. So can whether we prefer books, movies or television. It can be literally any kind of influence whether we're aware of it or not.

Individual perspectives can also come from what are known as *schemas* and *heuristics*. They are both psychological concepts that serve to organize what we know about the world and facilitate quick decision-making.

Schemas. A schema is a model by which we arrange and decipher the information we're currently receiving. It allows us to say, "Okay, based on these three factors I can observe, I know what this is." Imagine a schema as a snapshot of a certain situation, and using that snapshot to arrange unfamiliar information. A schema will help you understand that you are in a fancy restaurant, based on the tuxedos and golden toilets you see.

Introduced by psychologist Jean Piaget, we have schemas for all sorts of situations. Schemas develop throughout our entire lives, though they're at their most prevalent when we're learning about something for the first time. But while schemas are extremely useful, they can steer us toward unwarranted biases or errors. Of course, they are uniquely personal to us depending on our experiences.

Heuristics. While schemas help (and hurt) us in interpreting new situations, heuristics are more about how you fit into a new situation. "If this is the situation, then I should act in this way." A heuristic will help you know exactly how to act in that fancy restaurant.

We make hundreds of decisions every day. Most of them are small, ultimately trivial ones: what we'll have for lunch, what radio station we'll listen to on the way home, what grocery store we're going to shop at, and so forth, unlike major life decisions that could have long-term consequences. We simply can't evaluate every last detail or possible ramification about small decisions. It would be a waste of valuable time and mental energy.

That's where heuristics come in. They're mental guidelines based on past experiences that we use to make daily decisions that we can't delve deeply into. Think of heuristics as flashcards: they give us quick, abbreviated information to help us make speedy choices about daily decisions that we can't stop and deliberate over.

Schemas and heuristics they take less effort, energy, and time, and make everything simple. In fact, it forces simplicity upon complex matters, which isn't always helpful; they blind us to the nuanced realities that dwell underneath almost everything under the sun.

Everything in this section culminates in the fact that there are a million and a half perspectives one can have about anything—but you only start with one of them. To find reality, you need at least a few. You'll need to proactively seek them out, as they won't come naturally.

This is all to say that you almost never have the whole story. Try to see your perspective as one bit of information to evaluate, and then search for the rest of it.

Perception is Biased

Another way in which we should deviate from our initial instinct is our *perception*.

Perception is similar to perspective, in that they are both about the information you take in from an event or experience. But while perspective is about our experiences and they obstruct clear thinking, perception is about how what you see or hear is interpreted in a way that doesn't represent reality anymore. These are usually known as *cognitive biases*. Perspective has your own unique filter on it, while perception has your brain's shortcomings' filter on it.

Yet another way in which our brains and instincts fail us? You don't even know the half of it!

Cognitive biases are ways in which the brain seeks the path of least resistance and energy preservation. It seeks to jump to conclusions and limit information in the interest of speed over accuracy. It takes what you see and hear, however brief, and assembles a complete story.

You can imagine how this might lead to a lack of clarity of thought. If you wanted to take the quickest and easiest path to a destination, it necessarily means you are going to be missing a whole lot. It's as if the brain handicaps itself and covers one of its eyes so it can create a picture more quickly by having only half the visual field to process.

And yet, they do have their useful bits. Occasionally that eye patch is beneficial. There are three main instances where this is the case.

When there's too much information to absorb. We live in a time when there's a deluge of facts, data, statistics, stories, accounts—basically too much information. The overload can be exhausting, and usually contains at least some bits of info that are of no use to us whatsoever. We can become overwhelmed and paralyzed. So it becomes necessary to filter out the information that's relevant and retain only the parts that we can use. This is where schemas and heuristics we discussed earlier come in as well.

Cognitive bias can help reinforce that filter, and it does so in several ways. The brain tends to latch on to the most repeated or recently activated memories. It also tends to remember events or people that are strange or humorous, and notices more strongly when something has changed.

Now what do we do with that limited amount of notable information? The brain tries to find a story. But how can you build an accurate story with a beginning, an ending, and a few bits here and there in the middle?

When we need to act quickly. Sometimes, we're in a crunch. Decisions need to be made in fast order. If we let ourselves get bogged down by inactivity or don't react swiftly enough, we can fall behind or risk our survival. Cognitive biases can be helpful in that regard—although, again, not without potential hazards.

Cognitive biases cause us to fall back on the things that are most familiar and comfortable to us. We rely on the most immediate and available resources. We focus on the present situation, preferring to ponder that instead of the past or the future. We concentrate on things we can more easily relate to and eschew tools or assets that don't make as much sense to us. We strongly prefer solutions that look simple, thorough, and relatively risk-free, rather than answers that are overly complicated, vague, or unsafe.

When the clock's running low, this may be a perfectly reasonable course of action. And it's almost entirely fueled by cognitive bias. But since it comes fast and furious, there might be some clean-up you'll have to do once everything's settled down—but perhaps that is not always the most important priority. It's similar to a preference for asking for forgiveness versus asking for permission in the context of doing something you shouldn't be doing.

When we're deciding what we need to remember for the future. The final scenario in which cognitive bias might be of assistance concerns memory. If only fragments of our constant information overload are useful to us now, then even less of it will be relevant to us in the days and years to come. So again, we have to cherry-pick the things and details that we remember.

This process involves reduction. We'll discard some of the finer specifics of things and events and form broader, more general memories. We trim some of the multiple smaller events off and reshape them into a few basic key points. Maybe we'll pick out only a couple events and elevate them so they represent the whole experience.

In processing these new memories, our cognitive bias again defers to those that are most meaningful or familiar to the brain. It will also "edit" certain memories so they become more accessible to us, but in this process, certain details might accidentally be removed or inserted—so we remember it slightly differently than how it really happened.

Your biased perception can help you on a limited basis, but they are decidedly *not* the path to smarter thinking. Thus, we delve into three of the most prominent biases to understand how to battle them. Remember, they all seek to abbreviate information for the purposes of easy decision-making and increased retention—not accuracy.

The availability heuristic. The brain tends to prefer information that's most readily available or comes to awareness rapidly. If something simply comes to mind swiftly or is more memorable, we tend to attach an importance to it that it might not really deserve. It excludes supporting information that might be important to consider, along with countering details that might be used to argue against it.

For example, you might see the topic "tsunamis" trending on Twitter. You follow a couple links to recent news reports that say tsunamis are expected to happen more often in the near future. The reports are compelling. You feel a little nervous. You become worried that you'll be a tsunami victim. You start thinking that you haven't prepared enough. You get to the point where you think it's inevitable that someday you'll get swallowed up by a tsunami and there's nothing you can do about it.

In all this concern, you temporarily forget that you live in Kansas, a landlocked state in the middle of the United States where tsunamis never happen. Tsunamis require a large body of water and are best known for happening to small island nations.

That's the availability heuristic in a nutshell: you got spooked by a bunch of instantly accessible information that made you forget the fact that the chances of you getting swept away by a tsunami in Kansas are virtually impossible. When you are asked about your fears, you answer "tsunamis" and ignore the rash of home burglaries that might be occurring, or that you are in danger of losing your job. Just because something is available or notable does not mean it is important or representative.

Gambler's fallacy. This common cognitive bias magnifies the importance of past events in the prediction of future outcomes. The bias dictates that conditions and previous results point to the inevitability of something happening down the road—when in reality, each subsequent event is independent of the previous. This bias wants to create a cause-and-effect relationship where none exists. For instance, just because a coin has flipped to the heads side one hundred times in a row doesn't mean that it's more likely for the next flip to be to the tails side. There is no relationship between each flip.

This particular cognitive bias is called "gambler's fallacy" because it's responsible for a lot of out-of-control gambling addictions. Somebody betting on a football game may say a certain side will win because they've always done so before, or because they've lost so many times that they are due for a win: "The Packers are due a win this week after all the tough losses, and they are going to get it against the Lions!"

Forget that this guy would be a terrible gambler if that's the information he used to lay a bet, but it illustrates the point. The past history of the Packers-Lions rivalry doesn't have anything to do with how well those teams have played in recent years. The losses of the Packers in recent weeks doesn't mean their turn for a win is coming. *Just because something happened doesn't mean something else will happen.*

Post-purchase rationalization. This cognitive bias seeks to reduce regret, and it's based on a fairly common consumer behavior.

Say you're shopping for home theatre equipment. You go to a showroom and see a couple different models. One's extremely expensive, features a lot of bells and whistles, and takes up a lot of space. The other's a bit cheaper and smaller, but to the naked ear, doesn't seem to be much different in terms of quality.

You might be persuaded to buy the bigger and more expensive one because, since it's bigger and more expensive, it must work better. But it puts a serious dent in your bank account and is too big for your living room. And you might not even really be able to tell how well the sound's working.

If you employed post-purchase rationalization, you'd convince yourself that you made the right decision, that it's what you wanted to do all along. You tell yourself that you can indeed hear the difference in sound, and you do indeed need fifteen different plugs and ports. You might know deep down inside that you went overboard, but that knowledge makes you uneasy. Regret makes you feel stupid, and no one likes that. So you talk yourself into believing that you did the right thing and got exactly what you wanted. No more regret, just eating boxed macaroni and cheese for dinner for the next two months because you spent so much on new speakers.

This type of post-*anything* justifying behavior extends far beyond purchases. Remember clear thinking's biggest enemy, the ego? This is where it returns. We do this sometimes when we defend ourselves from others, but here, instead of trying to convince someone else, we are trying to convince ourselves.

So how do we work to improve our perception and avoid being led astray by our shortcutting brain?

Of course, you can start immediately trying to be aware of them in your thinking and take note of how your perception is likely focused on speed rather than accuracy. But still, that feels inadequate against some of these thought patterns that have been left unchecked our entire lives. There are a few specific mental exercises that can help retrain your thinking to be clear-minded and measured.

Practice thinking of alternative explanations. Instead of making a snap decision, alter your focus to accuracy and not speed. Take your time. Stop feeling anxious just because there is uncertainty or the lack of a clear decision. Don't write the story immediately.

Try to think of multiple reasons or causes. Reserve your judgment and stop jumping to conclusions. For example, if you're sitting in your favorite coffee shop and you notice a huge drop-off in business, you might think it's because the quality of the coffee has declined. But it could also be because more people are making their own espresso drinks, or because it's summer and more people are doing other things outside. Or perhaps it's that the prices the store is charging are keeping people away.

In a sense, this is like reverse storytelling. In life, we often start with the conclusion and try to work backward. Instead of filling in all the blanks and identifying only one path to that conclusion, try to work backward and theorize multiple paths.

You might try an exercise of taking a scene, a person, or any other thing, and observing five details or characteristics about it. Then, for each of those details, write down five possible causes that may have led that particular detail to be the way it is. Try to vary the potential causes you list, ranging from the plainly realistic to the downright bizarre. This will train your ability to create a story around every detail, thus giving you twenty-five trains of thought instead of the quickest and easiest for your brain to process.

Most of us think only linearly in terms of cause and effect. But that's ineffective at best to understanding a situation.

Reword your statements as questions. Think of something you consider a declarative, absolute truth. For example: "E-books and e-readers are killing literature." That's a pretty strong statement. But try rephrasing it: "Are e-books and e-readers *really* killing literature?" The mere act of turning it into a question makes your brain start looking for answers. Instead of a conclusion, you've opened up a line of inquiry.

"Well, maybe e-readers are bringing more people to reading—that's good." "They may be changing *how* we read, but they're not really killing how literature is made. Maybe I'm just overly sentimental about physical books." With just that one change to your statement, you've opened up your mind to a new line of inquiry and exploration.

Even the six blind men could have benefitted from this. Instead of the one standing next to the elephant's tail saying, "I am definitely standing next to a willow tree," the situation would have been much improved by asking, "Why does it feel like I am standing by a willow tree?"

Get behind and challenge your assumptions. Let's say you have a very broad belief about poor people: "They're poor because they don't want to work." Challenge that assumption immediately: "Do poor people just not want to work? Or do they really have fewer opportunities? They've been closing plants and stores in town for a few years now—maybe they don't have anywhere else to go. And it's hard to get the proper training for a skilled position when you can't afford it . . . What if there is something else that causes it? What if there are about fifty shades of grey to this matter?" Am I saying something that fundamentally depends on an untested assumption?

The harsh truth is that whatever you think you know about a topic, especially if it involves people's thoughts and motivations, you probably know only about ten percent of what's truly happening.

It's always best to be proactive about challenging your assumptions through self-interrogation and especially through valid news and information sources—including people who really have deep experience in the subject you're thinking of. It's uncertain where many of our assumptions come from anyway, so it's good to reevaluate them from time to time.

Remove your need to be right. The truth is a separate pursuit entirely from this, and sometimes there is a stark contrast because you want to feel a certain way about yourself, especially in front of others. Truth becomes a lot easier to discern when you take your emotional rewards (and punishments) out of the equation and simply try to determine what's *real*.

If you face opposition, it's just going to cause you to dig your heels in and deny, defend, and stonewall. You'll be seduced into caring more about dominating someone than understanding. You'll want to avoid that sour feeling of shame when conceding defeat to someone—anyone. Even if you're right, very few people make friends by saying, "I told you so."

Picture how a desperately stubborn person would act—is that similar to how you are acting? Could anyone make an honest comparison between the two? Hopefully not.

Even more so, explore being wrong and understand the feelings that are evoked. Play out scenarios where you are indeed wrong. What feelings will you feel? There may be embarrassment, anger, humiliation, or shame—but do they affect the world or your life? Only if you let them. Perception is only biased if you allow it to remain unchallenged.

Memories are Wrong

More frequently than we would like to admit, we are flat-out wrong about what awe think what happened in the past. Our memories fail us constantly, but we'd never know because they also rewrite themselves.

Just because our memories are capable of remarkable feats doesn't mean that they aren't subject to errors that are just as remarkable. A false memory is simply a memory that is real, which is neurologically identical to a real memory, but not based on something that actually happened.

In 1995, Loftus and Coan from the University of California, Irvine conducted a simple study to investigate how to implant a false memory by fusing it with an existing, real memory. The study involved a subject who was given descriptions of three true memories from his childhood and one false memory. The subject wrote about each of the four memories for five days in a row, giving a summary and any details or facts he could remember about each of the memories (three real and one false).

Over the five days, the subject began to recall more and more about the false memory, introducing details that were never there, and that seemed to stem completely from the subject's imagination.

He purported to remember everyone that was present, and even the emotions involved. He was adding onto the false memory, not realizing it was made up.

Weeks later, the subject was asked to rate his memories for how clear they were. He gave the false memory the second highest rating out of the four memories presented. He could provide vivid detail—perhaps because it was fabricated, so the details conformed to his idea of what the experience would usually entail. Memories could be implanted in people just by saying that they had occurred.

Memories, if they are not entirely false or fabricated, can also be influenced by things as small as suggestive word choice, phrasing, and vocabulary. An infamous study conducted in 1974 by Loftus and Palmer at the University of California, Irvine illustrates this effect.

Subjects watched different videos of car accidents at three different speeds. After, they filled out a survey which asked, "About how fast were the cars going when they *smashed* into each other?"

Other groups of subjects watched the exact same videos and filled out a survey after as well, but the survey instead asked, "About how fast were the cars going when they *bumped/hit/contacted* each other?" The estimates the subjects gave changed in relation to the verb used, which influenced the perception of speed and impact.

- Smashed = 40.8 mph
- Bumped = 38.1 mph
- Hit = 34 mph
- Contacted = 31.8 mph

This simple change in vocabulary affected people's perception of an event, and in essence, changed their memory surrounding it. How reliable can memory truly be when we are manipulated by such small variables? This was an event that the subjects watched on video—and the speed increased by nearly 10 mph when leading language was used, a discrepancy of 25%.

The ease with which false memories are created is why eyewitness testimony occupies such an ambivalent place in the legal system. Memories can change during interrogation, and sometimes intentionally. For example, Annelies Vredeveldt of the University of Amsterdam states that asking questions about a memory can easily take a wrong turn if you ask questions as simple as, "What was the color of his hair?" or "He was a redhead, wasn't he?" The first question assumes that there was a male, and the second question is leading and draws its own conclusions.

Eyewitness accounts are highly trusted by juries, yet highly condemned by judges and attorneys who know better. Researcher Julia Shaw states that to implant a false memory, "you try to get someone to confuse their imagination with their memory and get them to repeatedly picture it happening."

This means simply repeating a false memory or story to someone can cause them to confuse the false memory with reality, and eventually mesh them together with the real account. There is a very thin and blurry line between memory and imagination.

Eyewitness testimony has been questioned since Hugo Munsterberg's seminal 1908 book *On the Witness Stand*. He questioned the reliability of memory and perception, and the legal community has taken notice ever since. What's scary is that research has shown that juries can't tell the difference between false and accurate witness testimony, often simply relying on how confident the eyewitness is (Nicholson, 2014). Additional support for the distrust in eyewitness testimony has been found in analyses by Scheck and Neufel, who proved that eyewitness testimony was frequently present in cases of suspects who were later exonerated based on DNA evidence.

Christopher French of the University of London sums it up best: "*There is currently no way to distinguish, in the absence of independent evidence, whether a particular memory is true or false. Even memories which are detailed and vivid and held with 100 percent conviction can be completely false."*

Our memories are incredible, but the same malleability that leads to memory feats can also be exploited to show great flaws. The same sponge-like qualities can lead to wrong information and skewed perspectives. These create flawed thinking, not out of unsound logic or perception, but if you literally remember something to be different from reality, you're going to have some kind of trouble. The main goal of our brains isn't to be accurate or even helpful, and thus, it can be easily manipulated and tricked.

The Laws of Logic

A final element of not trusting your instincts is recognizing how the laws of logic work—or don't—in what you observe, see, and hear. Used correctly, the laws of logic will lead you to the naked truth. Ignored, you will be blindfolded by others.

Just like with cognitive biases, by nature, the laws of logic go unnoticed. It's rare that we dissect statements from a logical perspective, and that makes for habitually sloppy arguments and poor understanding. If something *sounds* credible, we deem it credible.

There's a funny, if somewhat cynical, piece of "advice" for people who are a little unsettled about speaking in public: "If you can't dazzle them with brilliance, baffle them with B.S." In this context, "B.S." does *not* stand for "Bachelor of Science."

We've all been in conversations in which we realize that the person we're speaking with is saying something *wrong*. For whatever reason, their words don't add up. No matter, they continue and it causes a cognitive clog in your brain.

They probably think they're making sense—they don't *think* they're trying to baffle you with B.S. But on the other hand, maybe they *are*. They might be trying to convolute your thinking with distorted logic and crazy talk. Whatever the case, you can't quite put your finger on what's rubbing you the wrong way, and thus can't form a rebuttal. They continue to gloat and build their argument on a house of cards.

The problem isn't with your comprehension or ability to think—in fact, it's the opposite. You're dealing with someone who is *defying the laws of logic*, and while your ears are taking it all in, your brain's not having any of it. That's what causes the confusion.

But for the most part, this happens by accident in normal, everyday conversations where the people are well-intentioned. We've all done it before. We get caught up in making a firm point, get flustered if we're not convincing enough, and end up making statements that don't seem to make any sense, because they don't. We spitball on earlier statements in an attempt to salvage an argument, and hope they aren't picked apart.

It's beneficial to understand the basic nature of logical thinking and construction. In the world we live, it's a crucial mental skill to develop. It helps us ferret out the truth and process problems. It imparts the ability to parse arguments and statements and know if they need to be dealt with. This is one of Aristotle's main legacies to the world.

As a quick example, a friend may be trying to remember the shoes they were wearing a particular day. They say, "If I was wearing sandals, they were red." So far, so good. They go on to say, "I'm pretty sure my shoes were red, which means I was wearing sandals." Well, that second part doesn't follow—hopefully an alarm has been set off in your brain. It just doesn't logically add up, and you're about to learn why.

Dissecting logical arguments sounds complicated, but the foundation of logical thinking is actually pretty easy to understand. The concepts are straightforward. They use sentence structure and equations to illustrate how arguments are or are not sound at their core. Understanding them breaks down to assessing the different kinds of statements people make in explaining a concept or an argument. Here, we will go over four of the most often used laws of logical statements—two of which are actually *il*logical!

Conditional statements: X -> Y. The first of our so-called laws of logic is the conditional statement. It is simply a true statement, to be taken at face value. We'll use a conditional statement as the core example for all these arguments—"If you feed my dog kibbles, then he'll be friendly to you." Just to make things easy to understand, let's assume in this discussion that this statement is *always* true. There is a causal relationship.

This is called a conditional statement because it says, "*If* this condition is met, *then* this result will one hundred percent happen." The condition is your feeding your friend's dog kibbles. The result is that the dog will be friendly to you. There is a direct cause and effect relationship between the condition and the result, and it only functions in one direction—there has been no cause and effect relationship established backward.

Once again, we're pretending this will always be the case—every time you give this dog a kibble, he's going to love you. Using this as a given, the statement is logically sound.

We also call the relationship between the condition and the result one of *premise* and *conclusion*—which are broader terms that can be used for other statements. If a certain premise is true, then you can expect the conclusion or outcome to be true.

These types of statements generally don't present as issues, unless someone is trying to pass off that the conclusion will always be true when it isn't. It's when you start to play with it that problems arise.

Converse statements: Y -> X. Now, consider this statement: "If my dog is friendly to you, it is because you fed him kibbles."

Is this true, given what we learned about conditional statements? If "If you feed my dog kibbles, then he'll be friendly to you" (X -> Y) is true, does that mean the reverse is necessarily true? Well—it's certainly a *possibility*, since we've determined that feeding the dog kibbles is a surefire way to win his friendliness. But is it the *only* way to make the dog friendly? Maybe you petted him. Perhaps you spoke to him in a gentle, friendly tone of voice. Maybe you played a game of fetch with him that made him extremely happy, and he returned his happiness with intense affection to you. Maybe the dog is in a good mood. Dogs do that.

In short, no, $Y \rightarrow X$ is often a flawed argument—an illogical statement.

This is an example of a converse statement: it reverses the conclusion and the premise, or the result and the condition—it is saying that the prerequisite is true if the end result is true. And it's turned the statement into a logical flaw. It's true that feeding the dog kibbles will make him your friend. But there's no indication that he's friends with you strictly because you fed him kibbles. There are other ways you can make a dog friendly to you. You've just caught someone with their hand in the cookie jar. Remember, a statement only has cause and effect in one direction—from condition to result, and not the other way around.

A converse statement is the direct parent of something called the *false syllogism*—basically, a false premise. Its fallacy is also exposed in making leaps of judgment based on misunderstood connections, like this:

- Dogs love kibbles.
- Monkeys love kibbles.
- Therefore, dogs are monkeys.

In this statement, the two premises might be true. But the fact that both dogs and monkeys like kibbles doesn't mean they're the same thing. The premise used for establishing the conclusion—mutual kibble love—is therefore false, as is the conclusion. Converse statements are where you'll catch people the most, because the cause and effect relationship isn't always examined closely.

Inverse statements: Not X -> Not Y. Okay, let's try this one on for size: "If you *don't* feed my dog kibbles, then he *won't* be friendly to you."

Really? That's the kind of dog you have? If I don't feed him kibbles—if I've run out or, you know, just don't carry kibbles on me out of habit—then he's going to turn on me? What an ingrate.

This is an inverse statement. It preserves the premise-conclusion relationship of the original statement but turns it into a *negative*: "If this doesn't happen, then this won't happen as a result." It assumes a deeper relationship between the two than actually exists.

Cause and effect certainly doesn't work if the lack of a cause means the lack of an effect.

Inverse statements are trickier, because not all of them are wrong. Sometimes they're right: "If you don't brush your teeth, then they won't be healthy." Well, that's true. But it leaves out that there are other ways to make your teeth unhealthy—constantly eating food that's bad for your teeth, for example (even if you do brush).

It could very well be that the dog rejects all who do not bring him kibbles. I don't know this particular dog's neurosis when it comes to being fed kibbles at the appropriate time; I suppose it's possible it turns him into a hostile, nervous wreck.

Still, the dog may be unfriendly for other reasons. Maybe he just got back from chasing a car that he didn't catch, so he's a little disappointed. Maybe he's in a bad mood. Maybe you've insulted him. Maybe he was recently neutered. There are plenty of things that can tick this dog off besides kibble deprivation.

So while certain inverse statements might be right, not all of them will be. Be extra cautious with them and don't take them at face value. Many things will try to pass themselves off as true statements, but you can begin to see that most of them are logical flaws.

Contrapositive statements: Not Y -> Not X. These are statements that negate both the premise and the conclusion, both backward and forward. If the original conditional statement is correct, then the contrapositive is also always true, unlike the converse or inverse statements. This type of relationship does exist both ways, because it's about a negative.

In our trusty dog food analogy, the conditional is "If you give the dog kibbles, then he will be friendly," and the contrapositive would be "If my dog is unfriendly to you, then you didn't give him kibbles." This is true. This is *always* true. There could be many reasons why the dog is being a jerk (see above). But one thing's for sure: if he's unfriendly, then for sure you haven't given him any of his cure-all kibbles. If you did, the dog would be more agreeable. But he isn't, so you haven't. Remember, that part is a given, so if the result is not true, then the given is also not true.

Another quick example: if you go swimming, you will be wet. What does the contrapositive statement sound like? If you are not wet, you did not go swimming. That certainly seems to make sense.

It can take a bit to decipher these types of logical statements, but once you do, you'll find that you can understand the truth of matters instantly. Our instincts make us want to skip over the details of these statements because they make sense on the surface. It's almost as if our instincts are working against us these days!

Takeaways:

- Your brain, instincts, gut feelings, emotions, and hunches are all liars. They aren't doing it on purpose, but they inherently function by jumping to conclusions, saving time, conserving energy, and valuing speed over accuracy. Their goal is to function on less information, and the less of it, the better. Not quite crystal-clear thinking.

- Your feelings and emotions have the ability to overpower you and completely color your thinking. But that's confusing feelings for facts. They are entirely separate things. Reality is in fact neutral.

- Your perspective isn't reality. It represents your subjective and unique worldview, but it's not objective, it's not reality, and it is destined to be skewed in terms of your experiences. Some of these experiences are solidified in what are known as schemas and heuristics, which are the frameworks you use to organize and understand the world.

- Your perception is biased. How you understand the world around you is probably biased because of how the brain jumps to conclusions. These types of jumps are called cognitive biases. They seek to create a story out of as little information as possible, in order to avoid uncertainty. Battling cognitive biases involves being able to tell stories in reverse, slow down, and shift your focus to questions instead of declaratory statements.

- Your memories are wrong. No matter how real and accurate they sometimes feel, a disturbing fact is that memories and false memories end up being indistinguishable to your brain. Factors as small as word choice or pointed questions can distort memories. Unfortunately, we depend on these memories to form our world views and perspectives.

- Finally, it's important to understand logical arguments—especially *illogical* arguments. This is how you determine the truth and validity of what is being said. We hear these every day but may not be able to pick out their logical flaws. You can think of these as a combination of math and argumentation. There is the conditional statement (X -> Y, true), the converse statement (Y -> X, usually a flaw), the inverse statement (Not X -> Not Y, usually a flaw), and the contrapositive statement (Not Y -> Not X, true). It's not just word games; it's understanding the foundations upon which true and misleading arguments are built.

Chapter 3. The Open Mind

"It is the mark of an educated mind, to be able to entertain a thought without accepting it." -Aristotle.

You'd like to think that people place a high value on being open-minded and, as Aristotle said, entertaining multiple thoughts without fixating on one—but sadly that's far from the reality. In fact, it's far from how we are wired as humans.

You only have to scroll through the comments of any social media platform or news website to know that people really aren't so interested in hearing what other people have to say. If there is a stance, there is an antithesis to that stance. Furthermore, agreeing to disagree is not an option, either. Even when there are no stakes, most people seem to feel tangible, physical pain at the prospect of changing their mind and absorbing conflicting information.

Why are people so closed-minded?

What causes this quirk of humans to hold onto what it knows as the truth, and habitually disregard others? Why do we stick to an opinion—any opinion?

Like many behaviors that emphasize immediacy over accuracy, we can generally use the survival instincts of the brain as a scapegoat. It may sound cliché to say at this point, but it's the truth that the human brain is still stuck in the African savannah about 10,000 years ago, and hasn't quite turned down its alarm systems for modern living. Certainty won, while hesitation was hunted down and eaten for dinner.

Being closed-minded is just basic humanity in action. It's not a mistake or glitch, it's actually an intentional feature of our psyche.

But beyond that, there are plenty of other factors that keep us from listening to others. Of course, we have the aspects we mentioned in the prior chapters of ego, false beliefs, willful ignorance, and overall resistance to objectivity. Sometimes we're just in denial and only see what we want to see (more on this later). Sometimes we don't know enough to know that we are wrong (more on this later as well). A general lack of outside perspective or experience can also contribute—how open would someone raised to believe that electricity is magic be to any belief system that is not rooted in magic? Someone else might confuse an anecdote as evidence, and remain steadfast in their belief based on that.

Additionally, people seek comfort and security. They prefer confirmation, rather than disruption. Being open-minded is uncomfortable and scary. At the very least, a natural inclination is to seek a path of least resistance and which allows them to save the most energy.

Then there are those whose closed-mindedness is just a part of establishing domination over others. They're talking to fight, and thus they never listen to gain a deeper comprehension of something—they only do so to figure out how they're going to argue back. They're rarely interested in asking anybody questions, and when they *are,* they're usually the loaded kind. They state their opinions as absolute truth, almost as bait to be challenged.

Finally, there are those that fear the slippery slope. This is when someone sees credible information that counteracts their beliefs, and refuse to pursue it any further because they're afraid of what they'll discover.

Consider the following dialogue, stripped clean of offending content and focusing on a slippery slope argument against open-mindedness. Bob is tied his belief to the occurrence of a certain event in a certain year, while archaeologists and scientists have suggested that the event they're talking about actually happened two years *earlier.*

Bob's response to this research was somewhat confusing: "Even if those scientists are correct, if I changed my belief about that date, then I would have to change *everything* I believe in. Because it would mean I was wrong about other events and other dates, and the result of all my calculations would be wrong, and my entire belief structure would be disproven. *So I'm just not going to go down that road.*"

Most of these instances of closed-mindedness can be overcome through patience, evidence, and gentle coaxing. Through a series of experiments involving circuits, light bulbs, and batteries, you might be able to convince the magic believer that electricity is not in fact a bunch of tiny fairies being forced into slavery. People are instinctually closed-minded, but not impossible to reason with.

But sometimes, a particular over-attachment to beliefs and opinions occurs that is particularly tough to overcome. This is a danger zone, and it develops because some beliefs are so important to us that they become part of our *identity*. Identity is even more important than ego; you'll recover your sense of pride being momentarily crushed, but a blow to your identity will make you question your self-worth.

The most obvious example is with religious beliefs—it would be accurate to say that people attach their identities to these various beliefs. In fact, it even becomes a way that we describe ourselves—*I'm a Christian/Muslim*, and so on. But it even pops up in so-called rivalries between fanbases of different television shows or technology companies—*I'm an Apple fanboy* or *I'm on Team Jacob!* To be told that Team Edward is the correct way to be is a blow to you as a human—your opinions, your worldview, and your life*.*

It's entirely fair to describe oneself that way. But there can come a point where one's self-identity can get *so* wrapped up in those descriptors that they dictate our emotions and crowd out rational thinking. In fact, it's a pretty good indicator that if you start describing yourself with a belief, you're not going to be so open about it. That can breed a belief of absolute truth, which is always accompanied by closed-mindedness.

Our becoming emotionally wedded to our opinions mutates them into indisputable facts. That's when they become dangerous. When our beliefs possess our feelings and we cement them as truth, we start to exclude, judge or dismiss the beliefs of others. Undue feelings of superiority take hold. And in that condition, it's impossible for *actual* truths—even provable, scientific ones—to get in.

Is there anything wrong with this? Not really. There's nothing wrong with believing in something strongly, of having faith in your convictions. There's nothing wrong with identifying yourself with beliefs. It's even okay to use them as sources of emotional comfort. But for our purposes, it makes real understanding and clear thinking extraordinarily difficult.

Whatever the level of intensity, *everybody* is closed-minded about *something*. However small, this rigidity leads to a world closed off to reality. If you prefer Apple technology to Android technology, you are creating a bubble in which no dissent is allowed. It doesn't take that many bubbles for you to become completely trapped in ego, comfort, security, certainty, emotional attachment, or dogma. It's a risky way of living.

This chapter will address some ways to actively keep an open mind ripe for clarity of thought. We'll address some of the mental traps and tendencies that keep us from doing so, and we'll look for ways to blast through those inhibitors and get to the heart of reality.

Battle Confirmation Bias

We have mentioned briefly confirmation bias throughout this book, but it's time to dive into it because it's really the first place we must visit on our way to open-mindedness. It's not only an important tendency that we must avoid, it's something that we engage in frequently without being aware of it.

Confirmation bias is rampant; it is when one only pursues and listens to information or evidence in favor of a certain belief that we wish to be true. In doing so, it causes one to disregard, rationalize, deny, or steer clear completely of evidence that disproves or challenges that belief. It's not necessarily driven by ego so much as it is a desire for wanting to be correct.

Confirmation bias is the ultimate stance of seeing what you want to see, and using that perception to prove a pre-chosen conclusion. In fact, it's where you start with a conclusion in mind, and work backward to make it your reality despite evidence directly to the contrary.

The simplest example is when you have a particular stance that you want to support—for example, that dogs are loyal. So you type into Google "dogs are very loyal"—obviously this is going to generate results about the loyalty of dogs, whereas if you type in (1) "are dogs loyal?", (2) "dogs loyalty," or (3) "dogs are not loyal" you would get a broader range of the literature on dogs and loyalty. This particular stance does not have any consequences, but confirmation bias can also turn life-threatening.

For instance, you may support the conclusion that you are a world-class skier despite the fact that you have only skied once in your life. Despite evidence that you constantly fell even on that one occasion, you explain it all away as "beginner's bad luck" and insist that you are ready for a double black diamond course—a type of course that involves steep cliffs that one could easily slip off of into oblivion.

You see other people's warnings as jealous, and you even find anecdotes from famous skiers about how they were amazing after only one class, ignoring the warnings of everyone else. You find a group of first-time skiers who advanced quickly for inspiration. All your detractors "don't know who you truly are," and "underestimate your abilities." Unfortunately, you end up persisting in the belief of your abilities, and you ski right off a cliff and perish.

That's how confirmation bias can tilt your interpretation of the world by restricting the flow of information. If you want to believe an opinion, then you'll feverishly seek out sources that will buttress your belief—even if it's false. And you'll ignore (No, I didn't see that!), deny (No, I refuse to believe that!), or rationalize (No, it's different here! *I'm* different!) sources that counteract or disprove your feelings—even if they're true.

It tends to lock us up in an echo chamber, where we only listen to a small number of the same voices and a narrow range of opinions, all of them in support of our view. For all intents and purposes, this is your world and reality; this is the majority view that seems to be the truth. With so many people (people *around* you, anyway) saying the same thing, how could you go wrong?

Though death by skiing is a fascinating phenomenon, an everyday example can help illustrate this better as to how we do it in our lives.

Enter Sally.

She's gone on two dates with John. After she returned home from the second date, she sent John a picture of a wedding ring that she liked, and also asked for the phone number of John's mother. John is rightfully horrified. But Sally felt that she was simply acting assertively because she had asked five of her closest friends, and they all told her to do this. She also searched online and find one source (meant as satire) that told her to do this, while ignoring all the other search results that told her not to be so clingy so quickly. An echo chamber was created around Sally, and it led to a detachment from reality and the situation at hand. Good thing John and Sally met at the date venues, and Sally didn't have his address!

It's never easy (nor much fun) to be diagnosed with confirmation bias. But once you realize where it's stemming from, it should motivate you to seek a course of action to lessen its impact: *argue against yourself.*

If you're certain of your opinion, then you should be able to identify the arguments *against* your opinion. After all, you know exactly what you are ignoring, denying, or rationalizing. The typical sequence of events is that you have your opinion, an opposing argument, and then your confirmatory reaction. What then? Continue that discussion. Make an honest effort to create a back and forth to see the merits and weaknesses of both sides.

If you give 100% effort on your own opinion, you must give 100% effort on the opposing opinion. Engage with it and ask why it exists. Ask about the different perspective that created that opinion. Question the evidence you like as harshly as you'd question the evidence you dislike. Hearing the other side of an argument will give you a much better ability to understand a different position, the different worldview or reality, and the factors involved that you never considered. Even if you don't change your opinion, you've opened up a channel that wasn't there before.

For example, maybe you're talking to someone who is bitterly opposed to the construction of a new park in your neighborhood that you support. You think a park would substantially increase the livability and comfort of your neighborhood, but your opponent doesn't think it's a good use of money.

Instead of trashing the opposing view, ask why the view exists in the first place. Maybe they feel the money's better spent on improving local roads; perhaps they'll tell a story of a relative who suffered severe injuries on a street that was in bad need of repair. Or maybe they feel that a park should only be built after other social services are fully funded and operational. Whatever their reasoning, try to get a story from them, and see if there's a solution you can work toward together.

You might find that you even start getting defensive with yourself in this process, but attempt to engage in this from a perspective of curiosity, self-education, and seeking knowledge.

An important step is to write these arguments down, so you can truly see for yourself what both sides are represented by. Try outlining your viewpoints, and then make up arguments *against* them. Provide the same amount of arguments for each, and directly address the corresponding ones. Flip your Google searches as we did with discovering the loyalty of dogs earlier. If evidence is presented, find it, and search for the opposite if it exists. Remember that evidence is objective, but reasoning and perspective is subjective—yours included!

After all this sweat and toil, you may find out that you don't really believe your original argument as much as you thought you did. And that's the first step to cracking confirmation bias and starting to think openly. It's the simple realization that you should leave a 1% buffer of doubt and uncertainty for yourself, and being 100% certain about something takes work that you probably haven't performed—as you know from Bertrand Russell.

Our refusal to hear the opposing side isn't a sign of inner strength or resolve—it's the exact opposite. If we're so wound up with apprehension about giving an ear to somebody with different points of view, then we're already powerless.

Follow the Evidence

As an extension of denying your confirmation bias, another aspect of openness and mental flexibility is to *follow the evidence*. Wherever it points is where you go. Inevitably, a narrative begins to unfold as you delve deeper and seek to understand. All you have to do is at least look in that direction without regard to how happy or unhappy it makes you.

You might find real evidence that supports your point of view—great. But you'll also find evidence that you don't necessarily want to face, the kind that offers cogent and reasonable arguments against your position. Even people who have devoted themselves to fearless truth-seeking might bristle at this kind of evidence and try to avoid it. To a certain point it's fine, but especially if it really pierces the shields of their cherished identity—religious, political, social, allegiance to a fictional movie character—they may try to sidestep it and turn it away.

You know what I'm going to say: That's exactly the kind of evidence you should need to follow and follow to its utmost. It's a deceptively simple task—if you can let go.

Treat all the evidence you receive by the same standards of reliability. All of it needs to pass the same sniff test. You must be circumspect of all evidence, and this means tending toward high-*quality* information more than high *quantities* of information.

Imagine an arrow points in one direction after you review some information and perspectives. This is a green arrow, to symbolize that it is correct. However, you are going to have to be able to pick it out from a multitude of red arrows, which seem helpful but really aren't. Sometimes it's more important to be able to eliminate those red arrows, as you can never quite be sure that you are indeed following the *green* arrow.

Beware of black-and-white thinking. Black-and-white thinking is easy. That's why people practice it. But it's also dangerous. Starkly contrasted, right-or-wrong belief systems are the downfall of modern civilization. Unfortunately they're not going away anytime soon, but to maintain a path of intellectual openness you must learn to avoid black-and-white thinking—and keep it from inserting it into your own beliefs.

Black-and-white thinkers only see two options for anything: "You're with us or against us." "If it's not Mars, it's Venus." "If I don't follow that red arrow, it must be this red arrow." If the evidence doesn't point one way, then it definitely points the other. The middle ground of *maybe* doesn't exist because it's more important for them to be certain than right.

But that's an error of epic proportions. If someone doesn't like the color red, it doesn't mean they like blue. One discovery does not necessarily rule out another, and there isn't a causal link between very many things.

Only a few truths are absolute, and they're the ones that are provable by evidence. But all other truths—more accurately, beliefs—are more nuanced. There's more to consider and think about when deciding what's true and what's not.

Most people, in their natural state, are not sharply one way or the other. The truth is the same. Perhaps the tendency for black-and-white thinking is because of the following point.

It's okay to be uncertain—it's not okay to pretend you know what you don't. Saying "Maybe" is a perfectly fine conclusion, and an opinion isn't mandatory. Being unknowledgeable about current issues simply isn't an option. Saying "I don't know" is almost *shocking* to some people, because they've internalized that statement as a sign of failure or some kind of shortcoming. *All* of the arrows you can currently see might be incorrect.

To avoid that appearance, many of us offer an uninformed opinion off the top of our heads. We think it's better to have *some* kind of insight—even if it's completely off-base—about something we don't understand than to remain quiet or express doubt. And then, as we do, we stick to that stance for no good reason.

Sure, uncertainty is uncomfortable, or at least can be. But it shouldn't be so disarming that we try to conquer it by finding something, anything, to believe. The fear of being uncertain is why people accept conspiracy theories or the rantings of a charismatic cult leader. They may be completely without merit, but they admire the *sureness* they provide. Even if the beliefs are absolute rubbish, they're better than having no beliefs at all.

Almost invariably, the information they're getting is ill-formed, unsound, slanted, and even flat-out false. But that doesn't matter, because they feel like they know something. It doesn't really even matter to them that they're not right—because it's important to feel *certain*.

Your biggest stumbling block in this situation is emotional. It is the emotion of anxiety you feel from a lack of certainty. You need to understand and believe that there's nothing wrong with being uncertain, that ambiguity is not an affliction. Some might even say that being uncertain or ambiguous is *exciting*, because it opens up possibilities. In any event, being uncertain is far, far more preferable to believing in something false.

De-stigmatize the dreaded three words "I don't know." You won't lose points in the eyes of others. In fact, they might even appreciate that you're the rare breed who doesn't feel they have to have a ready set of opinions about something they don't know anything about. It's much, much better to be unsure than to be misguided.

Just remember this: Your search for truth is rooted in a desire to *understand*. You're seeking *knowledge*—you are not necessarily seeking *answers*. The key to getting through that uncertainty is to accept the chance to test or confirm our beliefs.

Thinking "must" or "should". This is one of the leading causes of biased and closed-minded thinking. Like other shortcomings we have discussed, this leads to you looking at a set of evidence with a conclusion already in mind, based on how you picture something should occur, and trying to mold the evidence to fit that. It is when you expect the world to be different than it actually is, and it is the opposite of what you should do.

Must and *should* thoughts are beliefs that you unknowingly treat as fact. If they don't materialize, even after you see clear arrows to proceed another way, you'll still be hesitant to follow the evidence. For example, you could carry the belief that dogs "should" be friendly—how might this "should" hurt you if you encounter a wild dog frothing at the mouth with rabies? *Shoulds* and *Musts* masquerade as evidence, and for that reason, they are a red arrow to be avoided.

Beware of the Dunning-Kruger Effect. This was coined by Cornell psychologists David Dunning and Justin Kruger in the late '90s. Simply put, some people aren't informed or knowledgeable enough to know what they don't know. Even worse, they're usually over-confident in their own abilities because to them, there is little nuance and only simple questions and answers. The more they fall prey to this effect, typically the more confident they are in themselves.

Dunning-Kruger occurs in just about any setting where there are people who assume they know best. You might see it during a chess match, where a novice feels that chess is extremely simple—while missing all the behind-the-scenes planning and nuance. It's just not possible to follow the evidence if you have no idea what you're looking for (and you don't know that you don't know).

Dunning himself recently noted that the effect isn't necessarily fatal. Many people appear to have it simply because they don't know what the standards for success or accomplishment are, so they're essentially flying blind, but giving themselves credit for keeping afloat. Once people become *aware* they suffer from Dunning-Kruger and acknowledge it, they can always reverse its effect by learning what to do and putting it into practice.

There are a few steps you can take that will ameliorate the Dunning-Kruger effect. A lot of it involves things we've already talked about: being humble and realistic about your current state of being, not being intellectually lazy, and not thinking that you're above anybody else in terms of intelligence or accomplishment. The world is usually not devoid of complexity, so if you feel there is little nuance, then you are probably missing entire levels of analysis. To combat this, embracing self-challenge is a key, because it turns out that if something appears too simple to be true, you probably just don't know what to look for.

Labeling. This is when you, quite naturally, attach labels to people, places, things, and perspectives. The problem is that any type of label's purpose is reduction to a single word, and the abbreviation of information. These labels, usually not carefully chosen or given much thought, go on to form your beliefs. These are hazards with relatively accurate and descriptive labels—what about when you unwittingly use labels that are ambiguous, inconsistent, or inaccurate?

One big risk with labeling is that instead of describing the specific situations or perspectives in isolation, you create labels that are negative and absolute. In such instances, it's not about the situation in the moment, it's rather about making judgments about all future circumstances based on what you have just observed. It's similar to when we confuse feelings for facts.

Jumping to conclusions is a theme that underlies everything that happens when you don't follow the evidence. Sometimes there is no battling this, but the key is always to slow down. Try to honestly answer when you have been fooled and made incorrect judgments, and when you have failed to see the whole picture. Think about interpersonal communications and how many misunderstandings you have experienced in your life, despite your best intentions and deep friendships.

Battle Social Influence

If we can characterize confirmation bias and following the evidence as something internal that you must battle to stay clear and open-minded, then social influence is something external that we must battle. In other words, we must resist the influence of others and draw our own conclusions, rather than parroting those of others or being overly dependent on them.

None of us prefer to think of ourselves in this way—essentially a follower. We all like to imagine that we have *free will* and are actively making our decisions and determining out own thoughts instead of the other way around. If you're not a follower, that means you're a leader.

Leaders blaze the trail and set the path instead of the other way around. They are strong-minded and are driven by a set of morals and convictions. Above all else, they alone determine their thoughts. The truth, however, is a bit uglier. What we might define as free will on a daily basis is actually just us being influenced in subtle and subconscious manners by other people and the settings we find ourselves in.

Here's a simple example.

If you walk into your new job and you find everyone wearing magenta shirts, you are probably going to find a magenta shirt as soon as you can for the next day, despite the fact that there is no dress code and no one has ever mentioned anything about magenta shirts. Something in your mind will tell you that you should be wearing a magenta shirt, even though there are no rules about it and the people you've asked haven't mentioned it either. You might even feel uncomfortable if you don't buy one within the week.

We are heavily influenced by the people around us and the contexts we find ourselves in, to such a degree that free will is more accurately categorized as just another decision that depends on what we see and feel from others. There are two infamous, landmark studies that show just how much we are swayed by others and left closed-minded.

The first study that digs deep into the concept of dubious free will is the Asch

Conformity Experiment. This study was conducted by Solomon Asch of Swarthmore College in the 1950s and broadly demonstrated the compulsion to conform and "fit in" despite our best instincts and interests.

The study was relatively simply and asked participants to engage in a vision test. In each run of the study, there was only one subject, and the rest of the people present were Asch's confederates. They would attempt to influence the true participant to conform and act against their free will.

The participant sat around a table with seven confederates and was asked two questions:

1. Which line was the longest in Exhibit 2?
2. Which line from Exhibit 2 matches the line from Exhibit 1?

Below is what the participants saw and made their judgment on. When participants were asked this question alone, through writing, or without confederates who would provide a range of answers, they consistently answered in the exact same way: Obviously Line C and Line A, respectively.

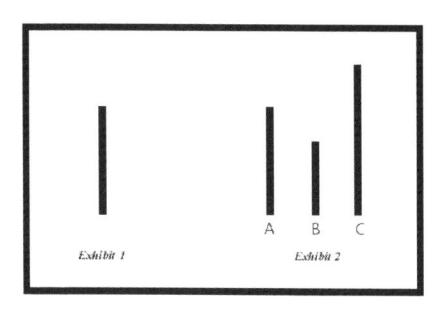

Exhibit 1   A B C *Exhibit 2*

However, when confederates were present and provided incorrect answers, what followed was surprising.

When the true participant was surrounded by confederates who gave incorrect answers, such as stating that Line C was equal to Exhibit 1, or Line B was the longest in Exhibit 2, they also conformed their answers to be stunningly incorrect based on the social pressures of the people around them. Over one third of the true participants gave an obviously wrong answer, presumably because of the influence of peer pressure and the general feeling of, "What could I be missing that everyone else is seeing?" This feeling of confusion and wanting to avoid appearing stupid can cause someone to conform to something obviously wrong, which will actually make them appear stupid because they were trying to avoid that very thing. Asch successfully displayed that people, whether they believe it or not, wish to blend in with their peers and their environment so they don't stick out.

People don't want to commit a faux pas, so even if they thought the line was truly the same length or not, they made it seem like they did. Asch commented, "The tendency to conformity in our society is so strong that reasonably intelligent and well-meaning young people are willing to call white black."

He had the opportunity to ask participants after the experiment whether they actually believed their altered stances, and most did not and simply wanted to go along with the group because they did not want to be thought of as "peculiar." Others thought the group's judgment was actually correct, and felt their new answer to be correct as well.

These two approaches represent the two main reasons people appeared to conform and act against their own free will. First, they wanted to be liked by the group and not seen as a "peculiar" outsider—this is called a normative influence. They wanted to fit in and be seen as comparable to the group. Second, they conformed because they thought their information was faulty, and they wanted to use the group's judgment instead of their own. This is called an informational influence, where they doubted their own instincts and assumed others had more and better information than they did.

In either case, people's clarity of thought is subverted by emotional reactions (discomfort, anxiety) to what other people are doing. You can say that you chose to go along with other people's answers consciously, but in fact, it wasn't what you truly wanted to do.

This is how we end up wearing magenta shirts far more often than we think we should. You might start with buying only one, but by the end of a year, you'll probably have a closet full of magenta shirts just because it seems like the right thing to do to fit in. You want acceptance from the group to not appear "peculiar," and you feel there's a reason magenta is so prevalent, one you don't quite know yet.

We take cues on how to behave and think from other people, especially if it's a situation that is foreign to us. For instance, if you show up at a fancy ball, you would look to how other people bow, stand, and interact so you can calibrate your own behavior. Where this takes a deviation into clarity of thought is where you go directly against what you know to be true just to conform. Asch's experiment was one instance where a clearly correct answer was passed over, showing the true power of peer pressure and social influence.

Stanley Milgram's famous electrical shock experiment chronicled in his 1963 paper *Obedience to Authority: An Experimental View* is one of the most important and famous psychological experiments ever conducted. And for our purposes, it demonstrates how we are slaves to authority and generally don't act in a way we want when ordered to do something under the guise of a duty. In more recent times, remembering the conclusions of Milgram's experiment can explain how atrocities as unthinkable as torture of prisoners of war have happened, or even how genocide was allowed to rise to prominence during World War II.

People aren't inherently evil and don't necessarily use their free will to inflict such harm. Instead, Milgram showed us another explanation as to why people can act in atrocious ways while still remaining very human at heart. It can serve as a general lesson on why people who are capable or who have done dark things aren't different from you or me.

Milgram began his research at Yale University in the 1960s with the initial impetus of studying the psychology of genocide. He began to theorize that people weren't necessarily evil, twisted, or even different from those who *didn't* commit genocide, but that it was rather a reflection of authority, orders, and the perception of a lack of accountability. In other words, if you were just being told what to do and you were conditioned to follow orders without question, there was a pretty good chance you were going to be able to do anything.

After all, that is the reason soldiers go through boot camp and are berated endlessly by drill instructors—it is a process designed to promote obedience and conformity, even in the worst conditions that combat will present.

However, Milgram's experiment showed it wasn't only trained soldiers who could fall victim to such blind obedience and have their free will taken away from them. Milgram built a "shock machine" that looked like a device that would be used to dole out torture, but in reality, it did nothing and was mostly a series of lights and dials. This would be his tool for exposing human nature.

His experiment worked on the premise that the participant was administering a memory test to someone in another room, and if the unseen person made a mistake on the test, the participant was given the instruction from a man in a lab coat to punish them with electric shocks stemming from the "shock machine." The shocks would escalate in intensity based on how many wrong answers were given. Before the start of the experiment, the participant was given a 45-volt electric shock that was attached to the shock machine. 45 volts was where the shocks would begin and then increase in 15-volt increments with each mistake. The shock machine ranged up to 450 volts, which also had a warning label reading "Danger: Severe Shock" next to them, and the final two switches were also labeled "XXX."

The unseen test-taker was actually an actor who followed a script of getting the vast majority of the questions incorrect. As the participant administered shocks, goaded on and encouraged by the man in the white lab coat, the actor would cry out loudly and begin to express pain and anguish, begging them to stop and then eventually falling completely silent.

Despite this, pushed on by the man in the white lab coat, a full 62% of participants administered the electrical shocks up to the highest level, which included the "XXX" and "Danger" levels. Milgram only allowed the man in the white lab coat to encourage with neutral and relatively benign statements such as "Please continue" and "It is absolutely essential that you continue."

In other words, the participants weren't coerced within an inch of their life to, in their perception, shock someone to unconsciousness or death! 62% reached the 450-volt limit, and none of the subjects stopped before reaching 300 volts. At 315 volts, the unseen actors went silent. The participants weren't being forced to do this; neither were they being yelled at or threatened. How could these results have occurred?

Are people just callous, with little regard for human life and suffering outside of their own? That can't be true. What's more likely to be true is how persuasive the perception of authority can be in subverting our free will. We will act against our wishes if we sense that we are being ordered to by someone who has power over us, no matter how arbitrary.

This obedience to authority and sense of deference can even push us to electrocute an innocent person to implied death. Suddenly, things such as genocide, the Holocaust, and torturing prisoners of war don't seem so far-fetched. We like to think we have hard limits on what we could inflict on others, but the results of Milgram's experiments showed otherwise—our free will can be completely bypassed because of a simple display of authority.

Milgram noted other factors might be the feeling that because there was an authority figure, they would hold no accountability and be able to say, "Well, he told me to!" When the participants were reminded they held responsibility for their actions, almost none of them wanted to continue participating in the experiment, and many even refused to continue if the man in the white lab coat didn't take explicit responsibility. Additionally, it was an unseen victim they had never met before, so there was a degree of separation and dehumanization that allowed actions to go further.

In the end, a normal person was shown to have followed orders given by another ordinary person in a white lab coat with a semblance of authority, which culminated in killing another person. It was quite the discovery in terms of what drives and motivates people. It was a very powerful piece of evidence that clarity of thought is subject to all manners of delusion and influence.

These experiments prove the simple fact that who we think we are doesn't matter. We can have the clearest of thoughts, and that also doesn't matter. What matters more in determining how we think and act are our surroundings, contacts, and the unique set of pressures that come with each context. Being open-minded means considering all sides, not deciding based solely on someone else's influence.

Takeaways:

- An integral part of crystal-clear thinking is to be open-minded. Being open-minded means to hear evidence or an argument and not make an instant judgment. It means being able to say "I don't know" and resist that feeling of uncertainty. These are all difficult because we are wired to do the opposite.
- The most glaring example of this is confirmation bias, wherein we are deaf and blind to evidence that doesn't support what we think. In other words, we see what we want to see, and we can make a belief appear out of thin air. This

is dangerous because it brings the ability to ignore reality. You eventually become entrenched in an echo chamber of reinforcing information that will definitely lead you astray.
- Confirmation bias is also the most prominent way that we fail to simply follow the evidence. If we perform research and keep an open mind, our task is simple: just follow the arrows where they point. But all too often, we are seduced into following the wrong arrows. These include the cognitive distortions of focusing on "must" and " should", black-and-white thinking, the Dunning-Kruger Effect, and labeling.
- The last way we must struggle to keep an open mind and clarity of thought is in relation to our social influences. The people around us can determine what we think and do, no matter how hard we try. This was proved in the Asch Conformity Test and the Milgram Shock Experiment. It doesn't matter how open-minded you are, your environment has the ability to push you strongly in one way despite your best intentions.

Chapter 4. Greats Think Alike

Diligence is the mother of good luck. - Benjamin Franklin (yes, again)

You don't have to take it from me. In fact, the basis of clear thinking would dictate that you seek to confirm what I say and discover further evidence to support my views on thinking. Thus, I urge you to seek out additional sources and perform your own due diligence. To that end, I have compiled some thinking methods of some of the greatest thinkers in history.

It turns out that many of them share this trait in common. When we seek to confirm information today, we seek verified sources or call on the work that others have performed. But often in the case of the majority of history's greatest thinkers, they themselves become the source material upon which people reference. They have nothing to guide them, or to point them in the right direction.

This means they had to define their own direction and methods of research in order to be able to determine *anything*. Combine that with whole new areas of inquiry, and you get a process that is necessarily clear and evidence-based. Just imagine that to many of these thinkers, they were setting out into a vast wide ocean where they had to set their own courses and draw their own maps; these days, we are sailing into pools with articulated lanes and directions for us to swim in.

All this is to say that none of these thinkers skipped any steps, and you probably shouldn't either.

Elon Musk & SpaceX

Although you wouldn't categorize Elon Musk as a "historical" thinker, he's well on his way with his growing list of achievements. He's certainly not responsible for originating this method of thinking, but he's applied it in publicly-renowned ways.

Musk asks the simple question: How can we be sure that we are not building our thoughts on a proverbial house of cards? Welcome to *first principles thinking*, which is stripping everything about a problem away until you only have the basic components.

Much of the thinking and analysis we do rests on the backs of other people's accomplishments, discoveries, and assumptions. We'll see how someone else does something—builds a bicycle, makes a cake, writes a song, opens a small business—and, more or less, copy what they did and just add a few things to improve it. We don't think much about them, and we follow suit for various reasons, one of which is "it's just the way it's always been done."

Another is that there's a result that proves it works, and thus why should we reinvent the wheel? We just don't give much thought to what underlies something that works, and we go so far as to trust that it's the best way sometimes. At the very least, it's safe and not prone to failure. This is a well-disguised form of intellectual laziness.

It may not be innovative or original, but following a proven guideline works. Or does it?

This is known as *analogy reasoning*, and it *works*, but is prone to errors and mistakes because you follow a path like gospel while underlying assumptions aren't questioned. Imagine if you were told that a cake has a certain amount of flour and eggs, and you simply emulated the recipe without questioning if it were true. This recipe may have been handed down for generations, but perhaps it was simply codified because one grandmother down the line only had so much flour and eggs available to make the cake. Perhaps this actually creates a rather gross-tasting cake, and if you deviated, you would improve the flavor and moistness tenfold.

The point is that what we think we know about a problem or scenario is often based on a set of assumptions. Assumptions aren't always correct. We assume that flour and eggs in a specific ratio create the best-tasting cake, but is it true? You just might be the blind following the blind. (Sorry to all the grandmothers.)

First principles thinking is the practice of getting behind this tendency to *follow*, and to question everything you think is set in stone and realizing that they are probably assumptions.

A first principle stands alone. Reasoning by first principles removes the impurity of assumptions and conventions. This method strips away the opinions and interpretations of other people and gets you to the essential elements that exist. From there, you can then build back up to a solution, often with an entirely new approach, based on truths that are unimpeachable and indisputable—because you are not resting on any assumptions anymore.

Thus, breaking Grandma's cake down to first principles would be to first examine what is actually needed to bake a cake and in what proportions. Only then could you start to recreate the cake to be tastier, and you might find that different proportions and ingredients are needed. It sounds like an easy solution, but sometimes it just doesn't occur to us that not everything is set in stone.

We also aren't conditioned for this type of thinking because of the sheer inconvenience it presents. First principles thinking is often discouraged, in fact, whether intentionally or not. Think of a child who keeps asking his parent a series of questions.

How do plants live? *"They depend on sunshine and sufficient irrigation."*

Why? *"They need the sun's energy for growth, and they need water to create food."*

Why? *"So the plant can conduct photosynthesis."*

Why? *"Because that's just the way it is, kid! Here, let me put the television on for you."*

That child is attempting to practice first principles thinking, although he probably doesn't know it. And his parent is shutting it down because, well, he doesn't really have time to go into it right now, it's too inconvenient. That scenario continues when we reach adulthood, whether it's a boss who bellows, "Because I said so!" or someone who says, "That's just the way it is."

Enter Elon Musk: the South African technology entrepreneur who is modern culture's most known and ardent champion of first principles thinking. Musk has been behind some of the most futuristic, forward-looking tech developments in the last 25 years, and espouses first principle thinking in everything he does. Musk has long resisted the analogy thinking that purports that something can't be done just because it hasn't been done yet. He fervently denies being told "that is impossible." Sure, it might be impossible according to their first principles and assumptions, but not *his*.

You can think of it as perpetually reinventing the wheel—which itself is a phrase mostly used to discourage people from doing so!

There is one particular example of this thinking method in action. When Musk sought to create SpaceX, a privatized space company, he quickly ran into the reason that all other privatized similar efforts had failed: the massive cost of rockets. Being that the business of SpaceX would be to send rockets into space, this was quite a roadblock.

But his price estimates rested on analogy thinking and the rigid thinking of so-called experts. He applied first principles thinking and broke down the real costs of getting into outer space, through buying a rocket or making his own. He quickly found that the price tag of the rocket wasn't what it seemed. Instead of buying a *finished* rocket for up to 65 million US dollars, Musk decided to *insource* the process, purchase the raw materials, and build the rockets himself. Within a few years, SpaceX had cut the price of launching a rocket to a fraction, by some reports 10% of his earlier estimates.

Musk used first principles thinking to break the situation down to the fundamentals, and simply asked what was needed to get into outer space. A rocket—that answer didn't change. But the rocket didn't have to come from Boeing or Lockheed, or any of the other established aerospace manufacturing companies. By starting from his goal and then identifying the inherent assumptions he wanted to break free of, he was able to create a more efficient solution. You start by asking, "What are we 100% sure is true and proven? Okay, let's disregard everything besides that."

To realize his concepts, Musk goes through a short 3-step process to blow past assumptions in the face of a problem to solve. For our purposes, let's suppose our problem is to recreate Grandma's cake with a lack of the ingredients in the recipe.

1. Identify and define current assumptions. These are things that appear to be givens, or unable to change. Grandma's cake requires a certain mixture of flour and eggs. Or does it?

2. Break down the problem into its first principles. Something edible resembling a cake must be presented. A cake typically requires X amount of eggs, and Y grams of flour. It needs heat and a container.

3. Create new solutions from scratch. Grandma's cake is unable to be created with the current ingredients we have, but we can find adequate substitutes for everything missing. What substitutions can be made in the recipe? Does it even have to be flour or eggs at all?

To see Musk's formula of first principles thinking in action once more, enter the *Hyperloop*. Musk wanted to solve the problem of fast and efficient transportation between Los Angeles and San Francisco. (Who doesn't?)

The current assumptions around such a solution are numerous. The obvious frontrunner would be a high speed rail system, similar to Korea and Japan's subway systems. However, it's an assumption that his new method of transportation would need to resemble any existing systems. What about reinventing the wheel?

The fundamentals of his problem were that he wanted a safer, faster, and cheaper method—it could conform to existing transportation systems, but it didn't need to. With those requirements, what kind of new system could be created? That's when the Hyperloop was born, and if you've seen pictures of it, it resembles an underground roller coaster more than a rail system. But that doesn't matter if the problem is solved.

You can use this model of thought for just about anything—building a business, learning history or the arts, even analyzing an emotional or personal issue. The problem or ambition doesn't even need to be that specific to think about it in terms of first principles thinking. Here is an example of how to use it for everyday purposes.

Your problem is that you don't seem to have enough time in your schedule to exercise sufficiently to lose weight.

Assumptions: weight loss depends on exercise, you don't have enough time, you need to lose that much weight, your schedule is too busy.

Fundamental principles: weight loss depends mostly on diet, you can make time if you stop watching so much television, your schedule still allows a few 20-minute breaks throughout the day, and you don't actually need to lose *that* much weight.

New method: A combination of short, quick workouts, and eating healthier by preparing all of your week's meals on Sunday.

Remember what we've been saying about clear thinking throughout this book: we seek to *understand*, not necessarily to find a complete and final solution. Just by going through the investigative process that first principles thinking espouses, one can see more clearly all the elements, individual components and parts of a situation. You get to see the ultimate truth in things. In some cases, this clarity of thought can manifest in creativity and innovation.

First principles thinking isn't easy; if it were then everyone would do it. But if you practice it long enough to get into the mindset, it can give you a whole new understanding of the world that nobody else would come up with. That's the ultimate goal of all clear thinking.

Darwin's Golden Rule

Charles Darwin, the naturalist whose theories on evolution and the development of species had wide-ranging effects on scientific study that persist today, was not a genius. He wasn't especially good at math. He didn't have the quick thinking often attributed to geniuses. Charlie Munger once said he thought that if Darwin attended Harvard in 1986, he probably would have graduated around the middle of the pack.

Biologist E.O. Wilson estimated that Darwin's IQ would have been around 130 or so—high, but not quite the level (140) where the word "genius" starts getting mentioned.

Instead, Darwin was relentless about learning. He devoured information about all the topics he was interested in pursuing. He hoarded facts and was hyper-diligent about taking notes. His ability to hold attention was legendary, and when it came to testing his work ethic was tireless. Darwin's thinking was purposely slow because he was so fastidiously detail-oriented. He believed that to have any authority on any topic one needed to develop deep expertise on it, and expertise doesn't happen overnight (or in a month, or in a year). The point is that Darwin is regarded as one of the ultimate examples of the importance hard work and diligence in surpassing natural intelligence.

Darwin's method was so all-encompassing that he even gave deep attention to information that countered or challenged his own theories. This approach forms the backbone of his *golden rule* as he expressed in his autobiography. The very basic guideline of Darwin's golden rule was to be more than just open to contradicting or opposing ideas—indeed, Darwin gave it his fullest attention:

"I had, also, during many years, followed a golden rule, namely, that whenever a published fact, a new observation or thought came across me, which was opposed to my general results, to make a memorandum of it without fail and at once; for I had found by experience that such facts and thoughts were far more apt to escape from memory than favorable ones."

Darwin completely immersed himself in evidence or explanations that went against his findings because he was aware that the human mind is inclined to dispose of those contrary views. If he didn't investigate them as fully as he could, he'd be likely to forget them, and that created mental dishonesty. Darwin knew that his own instinctual thinking could be a hindrance to finding the truth as much as it could help, and he established a way to ensure he wasn't missing out on any information.

Darwin handled all this conflicting information responsibly. He genuinely considered material that might have disproved his assertions, and took pains to fully absorb every single scenario, anomaly and exception to his theories. He didn't filter out information that didn't support his beliefs; he was utterly immune to confirmation bias. More than anything else, Darwin didn't want to be careless in finding the truth—he knew that a half-cocked assertion solely intended to persuade others without much thought was intellectually dishonest. Doing so required more time and effort on his part, but he was committed.

Of course, the Darwinian Golden Rule calls back to intellectual honesty and the maxim "Strong opinions but held lightly." It assumes intellectual *humility*, as being unattached to any stances or theories and simply following the evidence.

Uniquely, Darwin forces a dialogue of skepticism back to himself, instead of to others in defensiveness. To himself, he would direct questions such as: *What do you know? Are you sure? Why are you sure? How can it be proved? What potential errors could you have made? Where is this conflicting view coming from and why?* As you can imagine, it takes quite a bit of self-discipline to constantly double-check yourself.

Darwin accurately realized that if you hold the belief that everyone *else* is wrong, you're in trouble.

Another hallmark of Darwin's thinking was his exhaustive attention to detail. One of Darwin's biographers, David Quammen, states the following about his borderline obsessive tendencies:

"One of Darwin's great strengths as a scientist was also, in some ways, a disadvantage: his extraordinary breadth of curiosity. From his study at Down House he ranged widely and greedily, in his constant search for data, across distances (by letter)

and scientific fields. He read eclectically and kept notes like a pack rat. Over the years he collected an enormous quantity of interconnected facts. He looked for patterns but was intrigued equally by exceptions to the patterns, and exceptions to the exceptions. He tested his ideas against complicated groups of organisms with complicated stories, such as the barnacles, the orchids, the social insects, the primroses, and the hominids."

For eight years he studied and compared the similarities and differences of barnacles, taking to the seas on the *HMS Beagle* to discover the differences between individual specimens of practically immobile crustaceans. Most people, me included, would probably go crazy spending nearly a decade on finding the subtle differences between notably unexciting creatures who largely look the same, whose life goals basically center around finding a surface to permanently affix themselves to.

Darwin, though, had an unusual passion for this particular line of study. He thoroughly investigated each mollusk he came upon to find the smallest differences between each one. He sorted and classified the specimens he studied. He wrote his observations about mollusks *every day.*

Why? Because he was a glutton for punishment? Yes.

But also because he knew that his findings would be disputed if he didn't become an expert in his studies, and there was no other way to become an expert than to get intimately familiar with each microscopic feature and detail in his subject. The intense interest paid off, as his studies on barnacles proved to be a major foundation for his career-defining work, *On the Origin of Species.*

Thoroughness is truth, and there could be no delusions of ease or comfort in finding truth.

Along the way he found information that countered or qualified his own beliefs. But instead of disposing of them, he dispassionately and objectively studied every major and minor argument. Darwin knew he had to comprehend the arguments *against* his own theories more thoroughly than someone who made those arguments. This isn't how most people think, but if it's done well and with total dedication to detail, you can establish yourself as an effective thinker.

Descartes, Doubt, and the Scientific Method

René Descartes (1596-1650) was a French philosopher and mathematician, considered to be the father of analytical geometry and the source of great change in the philosophy of knowledge and scientific reasoning. He was also a devoted Catholic, which makes him an interesting case in the examination of the tension between science and faith.

Descartes was revolutionary because he felt that future progress in science would only be stunted by blind acceptance of the statements of his forerunners (i.e., analogy thinking). Most scientific thought immediately before Descartes' breakthroughs held firm to those old postulations, and he thought reliance on those old beliefs wasn't going to help anyone understand the true nature of existence. He had no interest in taking those old precepts for granted and went about searching for a method to establish truth.

Sure, they had persisted for centuries, millennia sometimes, but surely the understanding of the world had evolved in the meantime. A prime example as aforementioned is the Copernican theory of heliocentrism (the Earth revolves around the sun), which defied the concept of geocentrism (the Earth was the center of the universe) that had existed since ancient Greece. It took nearly two thousand years for the theory of geocentrism to be adequately challenged and turned over. Treating untested things as truths was problematic, to say the least—and to Descartes, nearly *everything* was untested.

For Descartes, the only unchangeable truths were mathematic. There was no questioning the physical precepts math provided: two plus two will always equal four, in this universe and any other. The area of a rectangle will always be its height times its width, whether local priests disliked it or not. But other science at the time was still subject to certain beliefs that, for Descartes, weren't quite established as fact.

What made them absolutely true without a shadow of a doubt? It turns out, not very much. So, in a burst of first principles thinking, Descartes sought a method to analyze evidence to arrive at solid truth.

The maxim Descartes established is the phrase he's most famous for: "I think, therefore I am," translated from the Latin "Cogito, ergo sum." His musings on it came about in his 1637 text *Discourse on Method,* in which he attempted to apply his approach to his own existence. It's how Descartes attempted to prove his own existence as a thinking being, by *thinking*. If he is indeed thinking, self-aware, and doubting, then that in itself is evidence of his existence. It's similar to saying "Am I being self-aware?"—the very act of asking means that you are being self-aware. In his own words:

"But I have convinced myself that there is absolutely nothing in the world, no sky, no earth, no minds, no bodies. Does it now follow that I too do not exist? No: if I convinced myself of something [or thought anything at all] then I certainly existed. But there is a deceiver of supreme power and cunning who is deliberately and constantly deceiving me. In that case I too undoubtedly exist, if he is deceiving me; and let him deceive me as much as he can, he will never bring it about that I am nothing so long as I think that I am something. So, after considering everything very thoroughly, I must finally conclude that the proposition, 'I am, I exist,' is necessarily true whenever it is put forward by me or conceived in my mind."

It's through that passage that you can truly see Descartes' approach to truth. Deduction and direct observation was the only true path to knowledge, and everything else from perception, hearsay, and assumption must be torn down and re-examined.

The process he established is what has evolved into what we now refer to as the *Scientific Method*. It was the first model for systematically seeking truth. Descartes framed his method as a kind of *cleansing*. He firmly believed the antiquated methods used by his predecessors left too much uncertain. So he established the method as a way to not just eradicate errors and omissions, but to prevent the potential of such errors being made in the future.

He articulated a few of his main tenets and we can compare it to the modern version of the Scientific Method.

1. Never accept anything as true until you can see it with evidence. Or, to restate: doubt everything and eliminate certainty. Until you can confirm direct and unmistakable corroboration of a fact, don't accept it—yet. Don't rely on the past assertions by others if they weren't arrived at through rigorous testing or examination. This rule also means suspending or eradicating all pre-existing attitudes and thought structures that make us jump to conclusions: prejudice, bias, snap judgments or lazy assumptions.

2. Divide every difficulty or problem into as many parts as possible. The complexity and complicated nature of a lot of problems can make analysis seem very intimidating, so Descartes advises dividing the problem up into smaller pieces. Rather than attack the problem in its massive, unified state, break it down into smaller pieces that you can handle more easily at once. Not only does it make it easier psychologically, you can be sure that you are proving the most basic truths you can find.

3. Start with the most easily understood problem, then take on the more difficult parts gradually. Take the most basic element of the problem, deduce to understand it completely, and then use that deduction to advance to the more difficult aspects. Use each conclusion that you've made to deduce the next one up. For unquestionable truth, you must ensure that each building block you use has been adequately proven. Descartes suggests this to make your thinking more methodical and organized, and to form a mental chain of evidence.

4. Bring all of the information together so it can't be refuted. When you've finished the thorough and systematic examination and come to understand the individual truths of your problem, synthesize all the elements and present them compellingly. Make sure to show that you didn't overlook or omit anything, that no variable or exception went unexamined, and that your conclusions are based on ruthless rationality, and even take into account all the attacks and doubts. As your algebra teacher told you, "show your work."

A notable part of Descartes' method involves his approach to doubt in the first step. By discarding everything that couldn't be established as true through unquestionable evidence, he was rejecting some beliefs that were, in fact, quite true. They just couldn't be absolutely verified by the scientific processes that had been used in the past. But Descartes was confident that by deconstructing all the parts of the problem and reconstituting them through his new method, those truths would emerge again—but this time with hard evidence to back them up.

The modern Scientific Method similarly restricts instinctive thinking and forces one to adhere only to the elements that are proven. Not much has changed over the years. Typically, it consists of five steps:

- What is the question you are trying to answer?

- What is your hypothesis about the answer to that question?

- Perform an experiment to test your hypothesis and find an indisputable answer. To this end, most modern experiments use what is known as *double blind testing*, which involves the experimenters themselves not knowing who has been subjected to what conditions to prevent subconscious confirmation bias.

- Observe and analyze the results of the experiment.

- Make a conclusion about whether your hypothesis was proven correct or wrong.

An intriguing sidebar to Descartes' innovation was his understanding of human nature—that in addition to being built for rational discourse, we are still only animals. We do a lot of things for survival that fill certain needs that aren't easily broken down by the method. Pursuing the truth with rigor and dedication is great and all, but you still have to eat, sleep, have a social life and hopefully a romantic partner. These are human needs that you can't always deduce through dedicated scientific reasoning.

You can't do any of those things if you live every part of your life by Descartes' rule of doubting everything. Human needs are built on our personal responses and desires, which are just as real to us as established truths. Descartes recognized leading a full, healthy life meant we had to accept these ethereal or visceral needs, and not subject them to the method. So he suggested being a human first—with occasional breaks to plumb the deeper truths of science and reality.

Einstein and "What if?"

Albert Einstein is known for many things: the theory of relativity, his contributions to physics, his distinct hairstyle, and that one picture of him sticking out his tongue. You know the one.

However, Einstein has in modern years become well-known for a few techniques that were said to aid his thinking and which led to some of his discoveries. Surprisingly, one he used frequently is one that we use most days of our life.

For instance, have you ever been with a friend and uttered the words "What if..."? You might be using this to explore a situation happening in your life, but what happens when you hear those words? Your imagination starts to work, taking as many factors into account as you can, and trying to project what would happen and why.

"What if humans were capable of flying?"

Most of the time, we're just doing this to spin our wheels and create new topics of discussion. But what if we used these for the specific purpose of gaining greater understanding?

Taking the effort to explore hypotheticals goes beyond simple thinking skills that require only memorization, description of an observable event or situation, or even analysis of facts and concrete events. Because hypotheticals pose questions about what isn't, what hasn't happened, or what isn't likely to ever happen, they challenge the imagination in new ways and sharpen practical intelligence. This is especially true when you pair it with a commitment to truth and clarity of thought.

For instance, you've never considered the implications of human flight because it's impossible, so there is a world of thoughts that have remained unexplored. For instance, how would traffic lights work, what kind of licensing process would be required, would we still have cars and airplanes, and how would safety work? Now, how would those rules and laws apply to normal traffic situations in the present day? What might a workable design include? How would gas stations work? How would this work in polluted cities? Think through the realities of how everything would fit together—it's no small feat!

Hypothetical situations taken to the extreme like this are more accurately labeled *thought experiments*, and Einstein in particular was known to use these. He called them *gedankenexperiments*, which is German for "thought experiments."

A thought experiment is playing out a "what if" scenario to its logical and consequential end, and trying to fit it in with reality. It's acting as if a theory or hypothesis is true, diving deep into the ramifications and seeing what happens to your "what if" scenario under intense scrutiny. Forcing yourself to reconcile something with reality will force you to more deeply understand what is involved and bring clarity to a situation.

A thought experiment allows you make new leaps of logic and discovery because you

can analyze premises that current knowledge (and reality) doesn't yet reach.
Flying cars may seem like a pithy example, but it presents many surprising considerations and problems when you truly treat it as something that needs to be accounted for.

Thought experiments lead to thoroughness, and remember, thoroughness leads to truth. Suppose you are carrying out a thought experiment about one that was mentioned previously: "What if humans were capable of flight?"

Indeed, what if? What does that world look like? Many problems are solved, but what new problems arise? What would your day look like if you could fly, in excruciating detail? What would happen to cars and airplanes? What forms of transportation would exist? How fast would you be able to fly, and what would it be based on? How does intercontinental travel work? Would the ability to fly stem from wings or hollow bones or a general supernatural power?

This is the essence of the thought experiment. *Suppose this happens. What happens next? What would that necessitate? And then? And then? And then what implications would arise? And so on.*

One of the most famous thought experiments is called *Schrödinger's cat*, which was first proposed by physicist Erwin Schrödinger.

In his thought experiment, he sealed a hypothetical cat inside a box along with two things: a radioactive element and a vial of poison. There is a 50% chance that the radioactive element will decay over the hour, and if it does, then the poison will be released, automatically killing the cat.

But in the 50% chance the radioactive element does not decay, the cat will remain alive. Because of the equal probabilities, it was argued that the cat was simultaneously alive and dead in the box at the end of the hour. That's odd, isn't it? Without getting into the weeds too much, this is a clear paradox because it is impossible for something to be in two different states simultaneously, being dependent on a random molecular event that wasn't sure to occur.

How could an impossibility like that exist under current theories? Well, it can't. Which means something is missing or needs to be changed. The Schrödinger's Cat thought experiment proved that there were constraints to current quantum physics theories and gaps in the knowledge of how they were applied. This never could have been something observable or testable, and a simple thought experiment was able to discover this shortcoming.

Thought experiments were one of Einstein's superpowers. He could imagine a scenario, play it out mentally with shocking accuracy and detail, and then extract the subtle conclusions that lay within.

One of Einstein's most famous *gedankenexperiments* begins with a simple premise: what would happen if you chase and then eventually caught up and rode a beam of light through space? In theory, once you caught up to the beam of light, it would appear to be frozen next to you because you are moving at the same speed. Just like if you are walking at the same pace as a car driving next to you, there is no acceleration (the relative velocities are the same), so the car would appear to be stuck to your side. So far, so good.

The only problem was that this made no sense with the then-current understanding of physics and relativity. If you caught up to the light and stood upon it, then the light would appear to be frozen right next to you like a car. But that means it's not light anymore as it was understood to be emitted in bursts at the time.

Similarly to Schrodinger's Cat, realizing that light ceased to be light meant that a fundamental rule of physics (Maxwell's emission theory of light) was either incorrect or incomplete. This thought experiment allowed Einstein to challenge the convention and eventually challenge what were thought to be set-in-stone rules set forth by Isaac Newton's three laws of energy and matter. Again, without getting into the weeds, this meant that the concept of time could not be a constant, which directly laid the path for the theory of relativity.

Descartes would certainly have approved if they were contemporaries. Einstein used thought experiments to test theories and so-called *rules* that were unable to be tested in the real, physical world. In the process, he found that he could pursue truth without having to lift a finger.

Socrates the Know-It-All

Finally, we come to the Socratic Method. It sounds like it could be an ancient Greek method of losing weight, but instead it's an ancient Greek method of discourse, teaching, and learning. As with the other thinkers in this chapter, the focus is on understanding and seeking truth.

When you boil it down, the Socratic Method is when you ask questions upon questions in an effort to dissect an assertion or statement. The person asking the questions might seem like they are on the offensive, but they are asking questions to enrich both parties and discover the underlying assumptions and motivations of the assertion or statement.

Imagine that you make a proclamation, and the only response you get is a smug, "Oh, is that so? What about X and Y?" Unfortunately, the know-it-all is on the right path.

American law schools are notorious for using the Socratic Method—where a student will essentially have to defend their statement against a professor's questioning regarding the merits of a case or law. Again, it's not adversarial by nature, it merely capitalizes on the fact that when you force someone to defend themselves or explain their line of thinking, they will often find gaps in their logic if the right questions are asked and emphasized. It may cause defensiveness, though it is not offensive.

As you might have guessed, the Socratic Method derived from Socrates himself, who is best known as being the teacher of the famous philosopher Plato, and also for willingly being executed by drinking poisoned hemlock for having "corrupted the minds of the youth" in Athens.

So what is the Socratic Method, exactly, beyond asking a series of tough questions that make people uncomfortable? You are putting what people say to an incredible stress test. When you use it on others or yourself, it trains you to question beliefs, discard assumptions, and find the implicit hypotheses people are operating on. You are discouraged from taking things at face value, and instead are encouraged and pushed to pick statements and assertions apart so you can find weaknesses and hidden intentions.

If you are mercilessly questioned and picked apart with Socratic questioning, what remains afterward will be heavily tested, validated, and rock solid. If there is an error in your thinking, it will be found, corrected, and proofed with a rebuttal.

As a brief example, imagine that you are telling someone that the sky is blue.

This seems like an unquestionable statement that is an easy truth. Obviously the sky is blue. You've known that since you were a child. You go outside and witness it each day. You've told someone that their eyes were as blue as the sky. Now, imagine someone asks *how* you know.

There are many ways to answer that question, but you decide to say that you know the sky is blue because it reflects the ocean, and that the ocean is blue, even though this is completely erroneous. The questioner asks how you know that color in particular is blue, and how you know it is a reflection of the ocean.

How would you answer this?

This incredibly brief yet effective line of Socratic questioning just revealed that you have no idea why you know the color blue is indeed blue, and why or how the sky reflects (or doesn't) the blue of the planet's oceans.

That, in a nutshell, is the importance of the Socratic Method. A series of innocent and simple questions can unravel what you thought you knew and lead you to understand exactly what you don't know. This is often just as important as knowing what you do know because it uncovers your blind spots and weaknesses. Recall that it was used by teachers on students, so it is designed to allow people to gain knowledge about themselves by asking the right questions. The questions are essentially tests of logic and knowledge so people may discover what they know and what they do not.

I wouldn't suggest doing this on a regular basis to people, at least if they aren't fully prepared for it. The reason is that this can easily be seen as adversarial and obnoxious. This is especially true if people can't answer your questions, and they realize their assertions are mostly assumptions they don't fully understand, and that their lack of understanding is being fully exposed. For example, how might you respond if someone soundly demonstrated to you that you don't understand why the sky is blue as the example above?

If you wanted to learn about it, it would be great. But if you just wanted to have a normal conversation with someone and they started a line of Socratic questioning, that's not typically a pleasurable conversation for the person in the student role, because they are continually on the defensive.

There are generally six types of Socratic questions, as delineated by R.W. Paul. After just briefly glancing at this list, it should be apparent how continually addressing these types of questions can improve your thinking and lead you to better solutions and assertions.

The six types of questions are:

1. Conceptual clarification questions
2. Probing assumptions
3. Probing rationale, reasons, evidence
4. Questioning viewpoints and perspectives
5. Probing implications and consequences
6. Questions about the question

Conceptual clarification questions: What is the significance and motivation for bringing up this topic, and why was it important enough for them to say? What do they hope to achieve with it?

Suppose we have the same assertion from above, where the sky is blue. Here are some sample questions from each category you could plausibly ask to gain clarity and challenge their thoughts.

- What does it matter to you if the sky is blue?
- What is the significance to you?
- What does that have to do with the rest of the discussion?
- Why would you say that?

Probing assumptions: What assumptions are the assertions based on, and are actually supported by evidence? What is opinion and belief, and what is evidence-based fact or proven in some other way?

- Is your blue my blue?
- Why do you think the sky is blue?
- So what leads you to believe the sky is blue?
- How can you prove that the sky is blue?

Probing rationale, reasons, and evidence: How do you know the evidence is trustworthy and valid? What are the conclusions drawn and what rationale, reasons, and evidence are specifically used in such a way? What might be missing or glazed over?

- What's the evidence for the sky's color and why is it convincing?
- How exactly does the ocean's reflection color the sky?
- What if the study was incorrect or flawed?
- Show me your reasoning.

Questioning viewpoints and perspectives: People will almost always present an assertion or argument from a specific bias, so play devil's advocate and remain skeptical about what they have come up with. Ask why opposing viewpoints and perspectives aren't preferred and why they don't work.

- How else could your evidence be interpreted?
- Why is that research the best in proving that the sky is blue?
- Couldn't the same be said about proving the sky is red? Why or why not?
- Why doesn't the sky color the ocean instead of the other way around?

Probing implications and consequences: What are the conclusions and why? What else could it mean and why was this particular conclusion drawn? What will happen as a consequence and why?

- If the sky is blue, what does that mean about reflections?

- Who is affected by the sky's color?
- If the sky is blue, what does that mean about the ocean?
- What else could your evidence and research prove about the planet?

Questions about the question: Forcing people to step into your shoes and ponder why you asked the question or why you went down that line of questioning. What did you mean when you said that, and why did you ask about X rather than Y?

- So why do you think I asked you about your belief in the sky's color?
- What do you think I wanted to do when I asked you about this?
- How do you think this knowledge might help you in other topics?
- How does this apply to everyday life and what we were discussing earlier?

At first, it sounds like a broken record, but there is a method to the madness. Each question may seem similar, but if answered correctly and adequately, go in different directions. In the example of the blue sky, there are twenty-four separate questions—twenty-four separate answers and probes into someone's simple assertion that the sky is blue. You can almost imagine how someone might lose their nerve and belief in the sky's blueness after not being able to produce evidence or understand the actual physical phenomenon.

The Socratic Method translates fairly easily to everyday life as well, though you must pick your battles. In daily life, it must be presented more as curiosity and doubt. Suppose someone makes the assertion, "Taco Bell is really healthy, actually." If you've decided that this is the battle you want to pick and possibly create a defensive and hostile atmosphere, you can.

Therefore, to the assertion of Taco Bell's healthiness, you could ask:

- Oh really? Where did you hear that?
- Interesting! The quadruple cheesy taco too?
- I've read the opposite! What's different about what we heard?

- What parts of the menu?
- Yes, I suppose, but what about McDonald's?
- What makes you say that?
- What nutritional standard are you using?
- What approach to health makes you say that?

You'll learn, you'll poke holes, and you'll understand. Isn't that what this whole thing is all about?

Clear thinking is tough, and these great thinkers show that disavowing the fast and easy path is necessary. Patience is a prerequisite, and the ability to use intellectual humility helps. Blind acceptance is frowned upon, and assumptions are meant to be questioned and prodded. The thing about clear thinking is that anyone can do it, but few are willing to do so.

Takeaways:

- Some of the greatest thinkers of human history have shared many similar opinions on *how* to think. That's no coincidence, and I'll trust them, especially when there is a consensus. Clear thinking starts with deconstructing what you think you know, understanding that you know nothing, and then building up from there. It's tough and tedious, to say the least.

- Elon Musk and his usage of first principles thinking is all about rejecting what is thought to be fact. He describes a process where you identify your assumptions in the face of solving a problem, you break them down, and then you solve the problem by breaking down old barriers. Once you realize that truth is not as set in stone as you think it is, possibilities begin to unfold. Reinvent the wheel—because maybe you can find a better one.

- Charles Darwin lived his remarkable life according to one simple golden rule: immersing yourself in the world of your opposition and contrary opinions. This is how you can legitimately test the truth of your opinions or arguments. It is the ultimate example of avoiding confirmation bias. He turns his doubts and skepticism onto himself rather than others, which is the far more normal course of action.

- René Descartes is sometimes known as the father of modern philosophy, and sometimes as the father of the modern Scientific Method. It was his usage of *doubt* as a tool that led to his significance in both fields. He believed that deduction and direct observation was the only path to truth, and thus everything contained a degree of uncertainty which was not tested.

- Albert Einstein is known for many things, but his thinking method of using thought experiments helped him discover the theory of relativity. It is a hypothetical situation, played out to the very end, as if it were reality. It allows you to test and study things that would otherwise be physically impossible, and make new discoveries therefrom.

- Socrates was rather a know-it-all, or at least that's how he would have appeared according to the Socratic Method. It was a technique of questioning a stance or opinion in a way to shed light on what was known and what gaps in knowledge existed. There are six types of Socratic questions: conceptual clarification, probing assumptions, probing rationale and reasons, questioning viewpoints, probing implications, and questioning the question itself.

Summary Guide

Chapter 1. Intellectual Honesty

- If you reflect for a second, clear thinking is not usually the goal we have in mind. We are usually after a combination of quick, simple, or easy thinking. However, none of those things are particularly *accurate* and won't lead you to the answers you seek. Unfortunately, it's what we are wired to do, and it takes conscious effort to slow down and be thorough. Most of the time, we also want to quell our sense of uncertainty, which leads us to conclusions that, while speedy, are not focused on accuracy. Intellectual honesty is about seeking plain and unadulterated truth.

- One of clear thinking's biggest opponents is the ego. This is when an argument, stance, or opinion is supported not by evidence, but by pride, the need to be right, and the desire to avoid shame and embarrassment. Ego keeps us deaf and blind if we allow it to. It serves a purpose, but very quickly becomes detrimental to your evaluation of the world, as it has the power to warp reality around you. The most prominent defense mechanisms we use are rationalization and plain old denial.

- Along with the ego, there are a few notable obstacles to pursuing truth and clarity of thought. They are intellectual laziness (*I can't be bothered to understand or research this, so I will accept anything*), willful ignorance (*I reject and deny that there is something further to understand*), and adherence to sacred cows (*that topic or stance is simply irrefutable truth; I refuse to question it*).

- It's easy to tell someone who is intellectually honest versus dishonest. It's all about how arguments contrary to their view are processed. The intellectually honest focus on understanding and following the evidence where it leads. The intellectually dishonest focus on a narrative that they want to preserve, and become defensive and sometimes outright hostile. The intellectually honest are able to answer questions directly and without justification; the intellectually dishonest must provide explanations, roundabouts, and deflections. Usually, it's clear that there is something being substituted for evidence that shouldn't be.

- Having an opinion is something we all do, but we must recognize that we often do it based on insufficient information and questionable evidence. An opinion is one thing, while forming a well-founded and defensible opinion is quite another. The latter, as Bertrand Russell writes, requires that you be wary of opinions which flatter your self-esteem. Imagine different biases and perspectives, look outside your immediate social circle, and question why an opposing opinion might make you react emotionally. It can be summed up with "Strong opinions which are lightly held."

Chapter 2. (Don't) Trust Your Instincts

- Your brain, instincts, gut feelings, emotions, and hunches are all liars. They aren't doing it on purpose, but they inherently function by jumping to conclusions, saving time, conserving energy, and valuing speed over accuracy. Their goal is to function on less information, and the less of it, the better. Not quite crystal-clear thinking.

- Your feelings and emotions have the ability to overpower you and completely color your thinking. But that's confusing feelings for facts. They are entirely separate things. Reality is in fact neutral.

- Your perspective isn't reality. It represents your subjective and unique worldview, but it's not objective, it's not reality, and it is destined to be skewed in terms of your experiences. Some of these experiences are solidified in what are known as schemas and heuristics, which are the frameworks you use to organize and understand the world.

- Your perception is biased. How you understand the world around you is probably biased because of how the brain jumps to conclusions. These types of jumps are called cognitive biases. They seek to create a story out of as little information as possible, in order to avoid uncertainty. Battling cognitive biases involves being able to tell stories in reverse, slow down, and shift your focus to questions instead of declaratory statements.

- Your memories are wrong. No matter how real and accurate they sometimes feel, a disturbing fact is that memories and false memories end up being indistinguishable to your brain. Factors as small as word choice or pointed questions can distort memories. Unfortunately, we depend on these memories to form our world views and perspectives.

- Finally, it's important to understand logical arguments—especially *illogical* arguments. This is how you determine the truth and validity of what is being said. We hear these every day but may not be able to pick out their logical flaws. You can think of these as a combination of math and argumentation. There is the conditional statement (X -> Y, true), the converse statement (Y -> X, usually a flaw), the inverse statement (Not X -> Not Y, usually a flaw), and the contrapositive statement (Not Y -> Not X, true). It's not just word games; it's understanding the foundations upon which true and misleading arguments are built.

Chapter 3. The Open Mind

- An integral part of crystal-clear thinking is to be open-minded. Being open-minded means to hear evidence or an argument and not make an instant judgment. It means being able to say "I don't know" and resist that feeling of uncertainty. These are all difficult because we are wired to do the opposite.
- The most glaring example of this is confirmation bias, wherein we are deaf and blind to evidence that doesn't

support what we think. In other words, we see what we want to see, and we can make a belief appear out of thin air. This is dangerous because it brings the ability to ignore reality. You eventually become entrenched in an echo chamber of reinforcing information that will definitely lead you astray.
- Confirmation bias is also the most prominent way that we fail to simply follow the evidence. If we perform research and keep an open mind, our task is simple: just follow the arrows where they point. But all too often, we are seduced into following the wrong arrows. These include the cognitive distortions of focusing on "must" and " should", black-and-white thinking, the Dunning-Kruger Effect, and labeling.
- The last way we must struggle to keep an open mind and clarity of thought is in relation to our social influences. The people around us can determine what we think and do, no matter how hard we try. This was proved in the Asch Conformity Test and the Milgram Shock Experiment. It doesn't matter how open-

minded you are, your environment has the ability to push you strongly in one way despite your best intentions.

Chapter 4. Greats Think Alike

- Some of the greatest thinkers of human history have shared many similar opinions on *how* to think. That's no coincidence, and I'll trust them, especially when there is a consensus. Clear thinking starts with deconstructing what you think you know, understanding that you know nothing, and then building up from there. It's tough and tedious, to say the least.

- Elon Musk and his usage of first principles thinking is all about rejecting what is thought to be fact. He describes a process where you identify your assumptions in the face of solving a problem, you break them down, and then you solve the problem by breaking down old barriers. Once you realize that truth is not as set in stone as you think it is, possibilities begin to unfold. Reinvent the wheel—because maybe you can find a better one.

- Charles Darwin lived his remarkable life according to one simple golden rule: immersing yourself in the world of your opposition and contrary opinions. This is how you can legitimately test the truth of your opinions or arguments. It is the ultimate example of avoiding confirmation bias. He turns his doubts and skepticism onto himself rather than others, which is the far more normal course of action.

- René Descartes is sometimes known as the father of modern philosophy, and sometimes as the father of the modern Scientific Method. It was his usage of *doubt* as a tool that led to his significance in both fields. He believed that deduction and direct observation was the only path to truth, and thus everything contained a degree of uncertainty which was not tested.

- Albert Einstein is known for many things, but his thinking method of using thought experiments helped him discover the theory of relativity. It is a hypothetical situation, played out to the very end, as if it were reality. It allows you to test and study things that would otherwise be physically impossible, and make new discoveries therefrom.

- Socrates was rather a know-it-all, or at least that's how he would have appeared according to the Socratic Method. It was a technique of questioning a stance or opinion in a way to shed light on what was known and what gaps in knowledge existed. There are six types of Socratic questions: conceptual clarification, probing assumptions, probing rationale and reasons, questioning viewpoints, probing implications, and questioning the question itself.

Printed in Great Britain
by Amazon